# LEARNING FUTURE LEISURE MARKET DEVELOPMENT TREND

## JOHN LOK

Copyright © John Lok
All Rights Reserved.

# Copyright

# Contents

# Preface

Introduction

Nowadays, on movie and opera art performance lesiure market, our leisures businesses have many different kinds to let consumer individual choice, for example, movie, opera art management, football performance, swimming , bicycle competition performance etc. indoor leisure activities. How can persuade audiences to buy ticket to see any one of these indoor leisure performance? We need to learn audience psychological factor and indoor environment factor if leisure businessmen hope to increase their audience number easily.

On future space city new tourism development market, space cities will not be science fiction, it will be achieved in possible. Whether what benefits it can bring to our future next generation. In this book, I shall explain what is the development differences between smart city development and space city development, then I shall indicate that what challenges to space city development will encounter , next I shall research view points to argue whether space city development is value or not as well as investigate what the actual aims to this space city development. How to learn space city tourism lesiure to let travelers feel more attractive to compare general earth travelling lesiure.

On airport indoor passenger staying shopping market, nowadays, global travel entertainment/leisure needs increase rapidly. Different countries people like to go to strange countries to travel. Exciting and enjoying travelling feeling is needed to satisfy to travellers. Hence, global airline industry service must be needed to improve to satisfy future global travellers' needs when they catch air planes to go to any countries to travel.

It brings this question: How to improve global airline services in order to satisfy travellers' comfortable and enjoyable catching air planes feeling in order to attract them to catch any airlines' air planes to go to any countries to travel often. I shall indicate some methods to attempt to explain whether what factors can influence airlines service performance or service level to be raised either better or worse.

On computer useful tool leisure market, I shall give reasons to explain how to develop future computer market. I shall indicate what factors will influence computer consumers' laptop purchases behavior as well as explain whether culture factor can influence computer consumer choice behavior. Also, I shall indicatw what service will be future computer related service need market.

In my this book,I shall attempt to explain how to apply audience psychological and indoor environment factors to help indoor leisure activity businessmen how to entertain to achieve persuade many audiences to chooce to buy ticket to see their performance as well as how to design new space city tourism leisure to develop new traveller market. Readers can have more fresh lesiure psychological knowledge to know how to operate leisure service business.

# Prologue

Is exploring Mars the most important factor
to influence traveller space travel lesiure choice

The comparison benefit
and risk between space
travel and space exploration

Mars exploration failure factors

Space exploration possible
economic benefits

What is space city tourism

Is Developing space city possible

Developing space city tourism aim

Chapter 4
Computer tool useful leisure Consumer Behavior
● Why China's computer manufacturing and product development industry will be global leader to compete US computer dominant market. p.61-83
  ● Factors influence consumers' laptop purchases behavior.
  ● Can culture factor influence the computer consumer choice behavior?
Bibliography and further resources
● Computer industry related service market development
● What kinds of technologies innovation products will impact our future lives.
● Autonomous automatic vehicle
● 3 D printer
● Massive open online course education
● Future computer innovative and sustainable food source market
Future computer industry market related business strategy trends
● Government ( public) and private partnership property development

strategy
● Online Tourism partnership
● Higher education marketing, enrollment,
branding and recruitment strategy

Internet market development trend
    ● What is Internet entertainment function
    ● What is Internet learning function
    ● What is internet for searching information
function
    ● What is internet for online office
Function
    ● What is internet for ecommerce
Function

Computer technology related service consumer
negtive emotion factors

● Technology negative influence reasons
Online technology negative influence
● How technology could contribute to bring poor standard
of living to influence our societies
How to avoid to technology brings negative influence on children
● Technology negative influence to low knowledge learner to feel difficult
to adopt future new technological labor market
● The negative impact of smartphones/ mobiles and desktop /laptop on
human health and life
Avoidance to driving and speaking mobile at the same time
What are the negative effect of electromagnetic waves on human brains
from smartphone influence
The laptop and desktop negative influence
Chapter 5
    Airport indoor travelling staying
shopping market
    Emotional labor factor p.84-100

Airports service environment
factor

Lean maintenance repair
and manual error factor

Influence of airside and off
airport to airport geographical
choice factor
    Influencing air connectivity
to service quality factor
    How to measure and rise airline
service quality

# CHAPTER ONE

# Movie and opera art performance leisure consumer psychology

What does theatre leisure ? Why we need to enter theatre to see movies or enter opera art performance hall to see opera art performance ? Theatre is a place where one group of people- on stage- tell stories to another group of people who are sitting... usually in an auditorium... usually in the dark... listening to, and watching these stories.Since human beings started to gather in groups and communities, they sensed the necessity to transmit their experiences and knowledge- fundamentally- through storytelling. The transmission of these stories, through the ages moved from shamanism to modern forms of art on and off stage.

Theatre is a tool that has existed for thousands of years. I imagine that from the first moments people wanted to transmit their experiences of the hunt, or their father and grandfather. It is both the wish and necessity of human beings to tell stories.Theatre is an art form that brings people together to celebrate, challenge and provoke through the telling of stories. Theatre is unique, you see transformation right in front of you- created in the moment. In a book; you pick it up, put it down and it remains – similarly with film- but with theatre, what you witness in any given moment is unique and only you and the audience will ever experience that.Theatre is a moment of intersection between people where events collide or reveal conflict through storytelling. It is an art-form that always has, and always will be, important and relevant.Theatre is a sense of escape, it transforms you into a new space. It can however, be many things. Theatre can be a source of intellectual learning, inspiration, and can even reflect your life.Theatre is live, and that's important. So much of our art is consumed through live-streams, through computers and so on – and this misses that extraordinary atmosphere, and sense of grounding and presence that theatre gives.

Why do we need to see opera art performance? Going in front of an audience- be it small or large- is a performance?you have to captivate people with what you say, do or whatever! This is the basic of performance.Not everyone can perform. The people who do it have a virtue that they can exploit to get that attention from people. Performance is about having the capability to captivate an audience with whatever means you can see with words, theatre, dance, music and so on.

What does leisure consumer behavior? How to persuade leisure consumer individual feels to enjoy the kind of leisure activities? I shall attempt to indicate art opera performance or movie lesiure example to explain how to persuade audiences feel leisure enjoyment to see the movie or see the opera art performance. For movie or art performance leisure, instead the movie or opera art performance, the artors individual performance attitude whether they can attract any audiences that they can feel enjoyment or leisure seeing feeling and the movie or art opera performance content whether they can attract their leisure emotion factor, the movie and opera art performance whole length of time factor is also important because if the movie or opera art performance time is too long, e.g. above two hours, then the long time movie or opera art performance can not persuade audiences to feel attractive, otherwise, they will feel boring when they feel that they need to sit more than two hours time to see the movie or see the art opera performance in the cinema or art opera performance hall. Unless, the audiences feel very enjoyment to see the movie or art opera performance.So, it explains why general movie or opera art performance time can not exceed two hours. Because instead of performance cost reason, audience individual boring feeling reason is another important audience leisure psychological factor to influence whether the movie or opera art performance can attract or persuade many audiences to choose to to buy ticket to see the movie or the art opera performance.

CINEMA MOVIE AUDIENCE LEISURE PSYCHOLOGY

Theatre is a collaborative art-form with writers, producers, directors, lighting designers, costume makers and so on. When all those pieces coincide, and when the performances are great, the lighting is great, the music is great, the design is great.... when all those different creative activities fuse into one emotional and intellectual delivery- that's when great theatre occurs.

Different films need to arrange different audience individual leisure taste to adapt their seeing movies or opera art performances raising enjoyment feeling.Each year a small number of new release films, 6-10 titles, become 'events'. These films such as the new James Bond, the latest Disney family feature and other big action titles such as the Marvel films or 'sagas' such as Twilight and The Hunger Games, are the bedrock of commercial cinema. These are mass appeal films created at huge cost and supported by massive marketing effort. They provide a disproportionately large amount of a cinema's annual income and they generally appeal strongly to the youth audience (16-24 year olds). 'Event' films are shown widely at multiplex cinemas but often perform poorly in local independent cinemas when shown a few weeks after the initial high profile release although some people will be prepared to wait if they have seen the film trailered at a favourite cinema.

In contrast a large number of high quality, independent and foreign language films are released annually but invariably they earn much less at the box office. These films appeal more to 30+ year olds and can prove to be very popular with particular audiences in individual cinemas. However,in recent years the 45+ age group has become one of the largest growth markets in UK cinemas with films such as The Best Exotic Marigold Hotel with more mature characters and strong storylines aimed at a multi-generational market. Young people, although still the multiplexes mainstay audience, are increasingly consuming film online through downloading or streaming services.

In fact, films based on literary works or specific aspects of social history or parts of the country are often well received by local audiences who prefer cinemas with comfort, character and the opportunity to have a coffee or a bar drink.Young children enjoy cinema going. Sometimes they attend with a group of friends. Often they are accompanied by parents or relatives. Films for the younger age groups are important for local cinemas and may attract sell-out audiences for morning or matinée performances, especially at weekends and during school holidays. Many cinemas now have a regular slot for this audience and operate it like a 'club' to encourage repeated visits. Local cinemas have to be capable of adapting to whatever is currently in the news and available to them. This requires skill and showmanship on the part of the cinema manager and staff in addition to a well designed building.

Why has theatre become such an important art-form?

In my imagination this goes back to the time when we lived in caves. I'm pretty convinced that two people, three people or one person sat on one side of a fire, providing the lighting- while a lot of other people sat on the other side of the cave or dwelling... and from time immemorial stories were told by one or several people, to a larger group of people. These stories may have been history, myths or legend.... they may even have been about religion or about grappling with the seasons.

Stories have always been told by live human beings to other live human beings, that's what makes it such an important and enduring form of art in my view.The unique selling proposition of theatre is the fact that there are live humans in a space, speaking to other live humans. It's not online, not in a cinema, not on some tablet... it's there. As a member of the audience, you are in the same space as the people who are- in the broadest sense of the word- telling stories. The very fact that humanity is at the absolute centre of theatre in tangible flesh and blood terms means that there is intrinsic beauty in that art-form because the human form, human voice and human ability to imagine stories (and their repercussions) is the stuff of art!

The aesthetic and beauty of theatre are very subjective. Performance and theatre can take many forms. It may be a play on the street or- as you saw during the early 19th century- a form of Opera where many forms of art were gathered into a single performance. The aesthetic of the elements of a performance when they are brought together depend on the culture of the people receiving it and where the piece itself is performed.The aesthetic and beauty of a piece of theatre lies almost completely in the eyes of the person watching.Theatre doesn't have to be beautiful. Some of the most fantastic and thought-provoking pieces are ugly. There is an aesthetic in the staging and design- which should enhance the stories or design of the production- but it doesn't have to be beautiful. Also, the notion of beauty in the theatre is- as in life- defined by the perspective of the viewer. For me, beauty may be defined by other simplicities... stripping away all the white-noise of circumstances and just focussing on human action. That's where I find moments of beauty in theatre, where those absolutely pristine quiet pin-drop moments occur... where the audience, story and artist collide in a moment of truth. These moments of beauty dig deep into an essence. Hence, we each have our own personal aesthetic- but for me the simplicity of storytelling and the collision of human events is where beauty and aesthetic occur in theatre.Theatre always has, and always will be, important and relevant.

## THE PSYCHOLOGY OF PERFORMING ARTS:THEATRE AND HUMAN EXPRESSION

Theatre is an arena in which we can mentally play, acting out our fears and fantasies in an experimental way. It excites new ideas and perspectives and provides us with rehearsal for life. In the broad sense, theatre can be taken as referring to films and TV as well as live theatre - indeed, any sort of entertainment that includes performers and audience (sometimes intertwined in complex ways) and which requires imagination to make it real.

Central to much of theatre is human conflict - the characters struggle to attain their ends against opposition, mostly from other characters. Role-playing puts us into the head of each character in turn, allowing us to see things from their viewpoint. By observing how they deal with their problems, sometimes adaptively, sometimes self-destructively, we learn lessons in how to choose among our own options. An important function of theatre is stimulation. Theatre adds magic and thrills to our mundane lives - whether it be disturbing (tragedy & horror), ridiculous (comedy) or romantic (esp. musicals). Modern civilisation has become overly safe. From time to time we need to rock the boat and test the alarms - to try out novel, challenging experiences and sample danger, albeit within a safe context. Theatre and films give us a chance to rehearse reactions to rare, dreaded occurrences such as rape, earthquake, fire or death of a loved one, helping us to cope with such events should they occur in real life. So, the audience leisure need difference between opera art performance and movie. Movie lesiure audiences visual enjoyment needs are whether the movie content is attractive or/and the or artistes their performance skills are proficient. Otherwise, the opera art performance artistes need have the actual time performance skills, because they need to perform to let their opera art performance audiences to feel visual leisure enjoyment immediate, if they can not persuade their opera art performance audiences feel happy or visual leisure feeling, otherwise, they feel boring when they are seeing their opera art performance immediately. They must decide to leave the opera art performance hall. So, all opera art performance artistes need know every opera art performance audience individual emotion, whether he/she is enjoying or boring when he/she is seeing their opera art performance on the performance hall.

What is the role of spectacle in performing arts?

Spectacle is largely a question of means, but it also brings an accent to a presentation or to the way of doing a show. At the beginning of Cirque, we were just a group of street-performers- not great acrobats, so the spectacle was little! As we went along, we were able to add artificial spectacle which was connected to the performance and enhanced with better acrobats- improving the whole experience. Now it would be very hard to go back to 1984 where we were just street-acrobats, people expect and accept spectacle from our performances now.

What is the role of the actor in theatre?

The actor is the person who tells someone else's story, he is the messenger of the story; regardless of whether that story was written by a composer, a lyricist or an author. He is the human-conduit to convey the story to the audience. His or her choices are therefore crucial in making that story as vivid as it can be. Also, the performer and his performance are the skeleton of our production. We can put muscles over this in the form of costumes and lights... we will add music, light and invoke the emotion of this skeleton by bringing it to life, but the performance is at the centre of all of this. Moreover, actors are communicators, storytellers, inventors and commentators. They have many roles in their art, depending on the story they are telling and the genre of the play. Actors are there to entertain, but also to deliver the story as the writer (or they, themselves) would want.As an actor, you are an artist. Greatness comes from the quality of the transformation, experience and how they can access and communicate emotion to effect a change in the audience.

Hence, theatre is an art-form that is meant to be heard. It is a collection of words and moments that are defined by the writer, but ultimately given voice by the actor. For me while it's always story first; the actor is the instrument for those stories coming to life. We each have our own notion of truth, but the great actors are the ones who make truth the through-line of their work. They are the ones who make the boundary between actor and character invisible- immersing themselves in the story. They are the ones who allow the audience to do the same. A great performance is not full of noise, but full of context and story. The actor must be generous, and give with abandon. Real theatre and real performance exists when you have a meeting of the performer and the audience as receiver. The audience are an active participant, theatre is a relationship between the production and the audience- audiences are not just consuming. For example, a piece of theatre is not complete until the audience is in the room. The work is changed by the presence of an audience. When you are making work you see rehearsals and so forth, but what the piece becomes when an audience joins the process translates it to another stage. Whether the audience know it or not, they are active in the process. They clarify things, deny things, join with ideas and more. Moreover, the audience are not passive consumers of theatre, it is a circular relationship.It is extremely important that an audience and a story become one. You often hear people describe the experience of 'losing themselves' in the story; I- personally- would call it 'finding yourself'. My guess would be that if you talk to the average audience member or artist, those unique moments that keep us coming back to theatre are relatively rare; yet we keep going. We want that moment where we get so immersed.. where all the people in the audience and the production come together... that is what resonates with us for years to come.

Designing a Good Theater to influence audience seeing movie or opera art performance positive emotion feeling factor

Instead of learning how to produce one good movie or opera art performance content and the artor individence performance skill and length of performance time arrangement factors, the designing a Good theater location factor will be one important factor to influence audience individual emotion. They may include as below:

Since humanity started gathering to tell stories and represent scenes from everyday life in front of an audience, the need for a space to perform such activities began to increase. Theater design developed from the open-air amphitheaters of the Greeks and Romans to the incredible array of forms we see today. Though some forms work better for particular types of performance, there is no ideal shape or size of a theater. The choice of the best form and scale depends on the functional purpose (movies, lectures, stage performances, musical presentations), the size of the staging required and the number of the audience to be accommodated. Let's see which are the basic parts that comprise a theater and the most common types of today's theater design.

1. Design a functioning Auditorium according to the type of performance and the number of the audience

It is the part of the theater accommodating the audience during the performance, sometimes known as the "house". The house can also refer to an area that is not considered playing space or backstage area. This includes the lobby, coat check, ticket counters, and restroom. The amount of space required for each auditorium depends on a number of factors but the following guides, based on modern seating design can give you an idea of the area needed

2. Keep the standard distance for a comfortable audience seating

The aisle is the space for walking with rows of seats on both sides or with rows of seats on one side and a wall on the other. In order to improve safety when the theaters are darkened during the performance, the edges of the aisles are marked with a row of small lights

3. The stage is important: choose wisely

The stage is the designated space where actors and other artists perform and the focal point for the audience. As an architectural feature, the stage may consist of a platform (often raised) or series of platforms. In some cases, these may be temporary or adjustable but in theaters and other buildings devoted to such productions, the stage is often a permanent feature. There are several types of stages that vary as to the usage and the relation of the audience to them:

Thrust theater stage :

A Stage surrounded by audience on three sides. The Fourth side serves as the background. In a typical modern arrangement: the stage is often a square or rectangular playing area, usually raised, surrounded by raked seating. Other shapes are possible; Shakespeare's Globe Theatre was a five-sided thrust stage.

For greater intimacy with the audience, go with the Thrust Stage

A thrust stage is one that extends into the audience on three sides and is connected to the backstage area by its upstage end. A thrust has the benefit of greater intimacy between the audience and performers than a proscenium while retaining the utility of a backstage area. The audience in a thrust stage theater may view the stage from three or more sides.

End Stage:

A Thrust stage extended wall to wall, like a thrust stage with audience on just one side, i.e. the front. "Backstage" is behind the background wall. There is no real wingspace to the sides, although there may be entrances located there. An example of a modern end stage is a music hall, where the background walls surround the playing space on three sides. Like a thrust stage, scenery serves primarily as background, rather than surrounding the acting space.

Arena Theatre stage:

A central stage surrounded by audience on all sides. The stage area is often raised to improve sightlines.

The Proscenium Stage or End Stage :

It is the most common type of stage and it is also called a picture frame stage. Its primary feature is a large opening, the proscenium arch through which the audience views the performance. The audience directly faces the stage and views only one side of the scene. Often, a stage may extend in front of the proscenium arch which offers additional playing area to the actors. This area is referred to as the apron. Underneath and in front of the apron is sometimes an orchestra pit which is used by musicians during musicals and operas.

Flexible theater stage:

Sometimes called a "Black Box" theater, these stages are often big empty boxes painted black inside. Stage and seating not fixed. Instead, each can be altered to suit the needs of the play or the whim of the director.

Keep your theater flexible

Flexible stage theaters are those that do not establish a fixed relationship between the stage and the house. They can be put into any of the standard theater forms or any of the variations of those. Usually, there is no physical distinction between the stage and the auditorium and the audience is either standing, intermingling with the performance or sitting on the main floor.

Profile Theatres stage:

Often used in "found space" theaters, i.e. theaters made by converted from other spaces. The Audience is often placed on risers to either side of the playing space, with little or no audience on either end of the "stage". Actors are staged in profile to the audience. It is often the most workable option for long, narrow spaces like "store fronts". Scenically, a profile theater is most like an arena stage; some staging as background is possible at ends, which are essentially sides. A non-theatrical form of the profile stage is a basketball arena, if no-one is seated behind the hoops.

Sports Arenas stage :

Sports arenas often serve as venues for Music Concerts. In form they resemble very large arena stage (more accurately the arena stage resembles a sports arena), but with a retangular floorplan. When used for concert, a temporary stage area often is set up as an end-stage at one end of the floor, and the rest of the floor and the stands become the audience. Arenas have their own terminology

Keep the scenery low for better visibility

In the Theater in the round or the Arena Stage Theater, the stage is located in the center of the audience, with the audience members facing it from all sides. The audience is placed close to the action, which provides a feeling of intimacy and involvement. However, this type puts major restrictions on the amount and kind of visual spectacle that can be provided for a performance, because scenery more than a few feet tall will block the audience view of the action taking place onstage.

4. Sound quality is as important as visibility

Although theater performances are a visual medium, poor sound quality will ruin even the better plays. The sound is an area often overlooked but, just as you need good sightlines, you also need good sound-lines. Apart from the obvious comfort and size considerations, External sound insulation (how many times have you heard traffic noise, trains or building works over the soundtrack of the film you are watching?) Internal sound insulation – this is particularly important with multiple screens where a loud soundtrack can leak into the adjoining auditorium.Services and equipment noise control – noises such as air conditioning, lifts, toilets and projection equipment need to be controlled. Acoustics – acoustic design in theaters should be considered from feasibility stage – location, auditorium planning etc. through to final commissioning.

What is theatre's economic role?
Every single independent tourist review that is written about reasons why people should come to the UK and London starts with heritage/royalty and then immediately moves on to theatre.... Specifically theatre.... not the arts, not entertainment, not shopping, not restaurants... the theatre. Alongside the fact that theatre employs many people in many diverse and different jobs, it's also a great regenerator of town-centres. If you speak to any government or local-government official that is trying to regenerate cities and towns further, theatres are at the centre. From time to time I get interviewed by an unnamed newspaper about the death of the West End. I always offer to take the journalist around London in a taxi where I can show them boarded up shops, boarded up offices, boarded up factories and boarded up pubs.
However, theatre is growing globally, and people want it globally. How the work of theatre develop will be a fascinating blend of cultures, it's an incredible opportunity. We currently have three proposals from Shanghai asking us to build, operate and convert theatres as a central core-magnet to retail, residential and other developments. This is alongside conversations we are having in Korea, Hong Kong and more. Around the world, more

theatres are being built now than at any other time in history. Theatre will lose the London and New York concentration. Hamburg, Vienna, Melbourne and Sydney are already great theatre cities. Hong Kong is growing into a great theatre destination too. There is also a huge opportunity across Canada and other territories. I see theatre essentially following an upward trajectory in terms of number of cities and venues.

People worldwide now acknowledge theatre is good for society economically and socially.

What does the next 50 years hold for theatre or opera art performance leisure need ? I think the essential core of theatre.... the unique selling proposition of being there to see it, having to perform in a space... will remain the same.... However what that core is saying and doing will depend on the message and story of the artists of the future. The activity of theatre has lasted for many thousands of years. As long as human beings have the need to hear stories, and to tell stories, it will remain. We're in very difficult times at the moment in terms of funding. This does however mean that we tend to get better at what we do. The work gets tougher, leaner and better. I would hope however that regional-theatre funding improves in the future, and we're left with a secure theatre network.

In fact, Theatre is ultimately about conflict between people and circumstances... you can wrap it in a different package and bow, but these principles have remained the same for hundreds of years.In the off-Broadway scene of the 1960s, you saw a trend of self-generating theatre in store-fronts and unusual venues. They were still going after the essence of theatre, but taking it everywhere. If you look today at the influence of technology in theatre, we are now able to do some of the things we used to do by hand- but more easily... for example, throwing a light cue by computer rather than moving dimmers by hand. However, technology gives us more tools to get to the core event, but ultimately the fierce passion the artist has to reveal the story is what powers the theatre.

How do artists cope with the mental pressures of perfection?

I would contest that we all have one or two 'issues' with our mental health, perhaps that is just the normal being of being a human. The discipline of ballet gives you the ability to manage your emotions, and an outlet for them. Ballet is a way to go through your emotions with the permission to exploit your frustrations, investigating them, using them and exposing them.Society faces dangers when people have doubts and questions, and cannot investigate them. When people hold-on to their emotions, and don't become malleable to them.. they become fragile, and can break, like glass.

What is the role of digital technology , how it can influence audience emotion from online movie or opera art performance online watching channel in the modern world?

Digital technology is making us insular. We think we have relationships through Facebook, Twitter and Instagram, but they are not real. There is no physical connection. We are human, we need physical connection. Participating in public performance, where you are a part of something with other people is more important than ever. It's more important than ever that we encourage young people into the arts in a meaningful way where they feel they want to go, and can afford to go. Right now, we can't even get young people through the door- and that's hard.

Looking even further to the future, we are entering the world of artificial intelligence and robotics. There is a chance that machines will be performing many of our world's most physical tasks. Wouldn't it be better if we guarantee the future of our children with creativity? That's the one thing machines can't compete with us on. Human beings will live maybe 100 years, and we leave school when we're 16, 17, 18. We need to teach kids to enjoy learning, to be curious, and to always want to learn. Not one iota of what they will become can be taught by us. The most important thing is that children enjoy the process of discovery. The more we encourage creativity, the more digital technology encourage young age audience group to imagine alternate realities when they can see movie or opera art performance from internet channel, the more our futures will all be brighter.

How has art changed your world-view?

Art has changed my world-view completely. I have travelled the world, not for tourism but to work. I have worked with so many different people, from so many different cultures and backgrounds and I have had my mind opened about humanity.I don't feel that I am a particular person from a particular part of the world. I was born somewhere, grew-up somewhere else, and lived in a few more places. I am a person of the world. Art has allowed me to live with myself, and to make sense of the fragility of humanity's desires and traits. I'm just a human being, and art has given me the space to be OK with that.

What inspires you as an artist? How you are as artist , you feel you may perform your movie or opera art performance to attract audience attention? Working with choreographers and producing stuff that really makes people think, and changes their ideas, and takes them to another place... that's powerful for me. for dance performance example, dance in itself is a social skill that everybody should appreciate and enjoy, our bodies are made to move. If you choose to specialise in the field- you're like an athlete. You have to be built for the technique. The role of the body is important and for dancers, it's about the joints, flexibility and muscular strength. The proportions of the body are also important; that's part of the aesthetic, and you can't help that- this is a visual art. How would be your art performance message to the next generation? You really have to devote your life to theatre. It doesn't mean you can't have a family and so forth... but it isn't like some activities in life where you can get a healthy work-life balance, as much as we would like to encourage it. Theatre is your life as well as your work, and if that doesn't fit with you, then theatre isn't right for you. Whatever your talent... music, movement, whatever... if you have the drive to continue and develop and become a great performer then you should. It's a lot of work- my father used to tell me that in life you need a little bit of talent, but lots of hard work. If you have a little talent, prepare yourself for hard work to develop it, and you may attain greatness; but don't forget that the road to greatness is long. You should make the work that tells the stories you feel are important to you and your generation. The role of a theatre maker is to tell the stories of our lives. You should try and grab the whole of the gamut of emotions, it's not just to entertain. The mix and bravery by which you grab those emotions makes theatre exciting. Moreover, you must be fearless and brave. You must be willing to express what you feel, and to do that with thought. People have a fear of expression, and we must encourage them to do the hard, hard work it takes to overcome this and know they are empowered to make work. All great work comes from this principle, new forms are made, new theatre is created.... When someone stops to write... or stops to raise some money? those are the moments where greatness is created. Also, you have to be curious and learn as much as you can from as many people as you can. You can even learn from people who don't know what they're doing; at least you will then know how not to do something. You have to be kind to yourself. You do not have to suffer or punish yourself to be a great artist. The sooner you can accept yourself, the sooner you can progress and discover what you're capable of. Life is so short, and goes so fast, you have to enjoy it. Life will throw you in so many directions, and goals are not the end; they are simply gateways to more questions, and this process of discovering answers and new questions is never complete, that's life. People have a lot of inhibitions, and are hugely preoccupied with what other people are thinking. Dance gives you a space to forget that, and enjoy being you. I always think you should dance with others, but it's amazing how happy you can be dancing on your own. For me however, the entertainment and enjoyment is dancing with friends or even strangers. Dancing breaks-down so many barriers, and makes you more comfortable with people around you. People let their guard-down when they dance, and it opens a lot of doors for communications. I have a fitness and dance programme that we take into state-schools. We let kids try anything they want in dance and let their creativity flow. They can do any genre from around the world- the aim is to find something that they can connect with to give them a feel of what dance can do. When you see the reaction? My God, it's the happiest they've ever been! They're testing their bodies like they've never done before, and finding skills that they didn't think they had. It gives them a space to enjoy being themselves, without peer-pressure, without the stresses that can impact their lives so negatively at this early stage.

However, art is one of the most valuable assets of human society, yet the truth is that while we may attach art to a time and a place; it's true provenance and relevance remain intangible. We can look at the raw materials (the paint, the instrument?, the composition (the brush strokes, the music) or even the act of consumption (viewing, listing? – but the thing that we observe only becomes art within us. The phenomenon of art emerges within the intangible mix of experience and cultural inputs that create our mind. A fact not lost on the ancient Greeks who simultaneously originated the concepts of philosophy (the love of wisdom) and theatre (the place for viewing) c.6th century B.C.

The images of other arts are constituted in quite different ways. This engagement has a metaphysical aspect in that the image between the performer and the audience adds up to more than the sum of its various parts. A materialist criticism that does not recognise these 'metaphysical' qualities of theatre is lacking critical force. For the 'beyond physical', the numinous, the spirit, the aura of art, however it is described is a material response to art not just ideological or 'imagined'. This 'something more' than the thing itself is attested to by too many people without deference to gender, race or class. And to ignore it, as though it will go away, and leave us with the quantified, the material and the manipulable, in the name of dogmatic sectarian objectives, is to impoverish the terms on which theatre might be most valuably and pleasurably thought and practiced. This metaphysics of theatre is what is not seen, beyond the practiced, beyond the mind's eye it remains unwritten. It is the domain which both makes theatre worthwhile and simultaneously jeopardises its effects. For it is in this hinterland of the undocumented and discreet that the fallacies of theatre are nourished. This 'something more' of the image does not disconnect the experience of theatre from its place of performance, nor from the everyday. Theatre remains bound by its context precisely through the unique relationship images create between audience, performer and everyday life." He adds that, "To value theatre, is to value life, not to escape from it. The everyday is at once the most habitual and demanding dimension of life which theatre has most responsibility to. Theatre does not tease people out of their everyday lives like other expressions of wish fulfilment but reminds them who they are and what is worth living and changing in their lives every day." (Theatre and Every Day Life, 1993)

The concept of everyday life here is critical. Human beings are cursed with the knowledge of agency. We know without a shadow of a doubt that our immediate experiences are limited simply to ourselves. In many philosophies this is even manifest as the discussion of how one is trapped in the body- able to only experience the substantive world which we have ingested through our limited senses. With this in mind, we quickly see the real power of theatre. Prof. Erin Hurley describes how, "Theatre allows for and offers vicarious experience: the experience of someone else experiencing something?We know that witnessing another's actions and emotional experiences can create the same neurological imprint as doing or feeling them oneself. Joseph Roach provocatively recasts the history of theatre in terms of the good of what he calls 'synthetic experience', a cognate to vicarious experience. The theatre is a port of entry into another's life and another kind of living." (Theatre and Feeling, 2010)

On conclusion, art is the medium by which we- as human beings- are able to relate to each other. Art allows us to understand things that are more than ourselves, and imagine life through the agency of others. Theatre- as perhaps the most human of all the arts- has the profound ability to engage us immediately in the experience of someone else's agency- at any point in time, at any place. It breaks down the loneliness of being a self, and allows one to realise that not only are there others- but that the self can be them too. Art Business Charity conflict creativity culture. So, any movie or opera art performance businessmen need to educate our next generation needs to considerate art performance movie or opera art performance lesisure industry needs to be continued to develop in order to let they can learn more new art culture and build positive charter role in our society, then crimes number will be influenced to reduce when they can see any health movie or opera art performance after they buy tickets to enter cinemas or opera art performance hall and let they feel that it is valuable economic spending time to see the movie or the opera art leisure performance.

# CHAPTER TWO

# Publish Market Reader behavior

Nowadays, publish market includes these main book service aspects to let readers enjoy reading interest, such as ebooks online reading channel, traditional book shop books purchase channel, library books lending service. I shall analyze how these books leading or borrowing and send hand or new books purchase choice to influence readers reading behavioral need change.

● Library Services in the Digital Age

The internet has already had a major impact on how people find and access information, and now the rising popularity of e-books is helping transform Americans' reading habits. In this changing landscape, public libraries are trying to adjust their services to these new realities while still serving the needs of patrons who rely on more traditional resources. In a new survey of Americans' attitudes and expectations for public libraries, the Pew Research Center's Internet & American Life Project finds that many library patrons are eager to see libraries' digital services expand, yet also feel that print books remain important in the digital age.

The availability of free computers and internet access now rivals book lending and reference expertise as a vital service of libraries. In a national survey of Americans ages 16 and older:

1. 80% of Americans say borrowing books is a "very important" service libraries provide.

2. 80% say reference librarians are a "very important" service of libraries.

3. 77% say free access to computers and the internet is a "very important" service of libraries.

Moreover, a notable share of Americans say they would embrace even wider uses of technology at libraries such as: Online research services allowing patrons to pose questions and get answers from librarians: 37% of Americans ages 16 and older would "very likely" use an "ask a librarian" type of service, and another 36% say they would be "somewhat likely" to do so.

Apps-based access to library materials and programs: 35% of Americans ages 16 and older would "very likely" use that service and another 28% say they would be "somewhat likely" to do so.

Access to technology "petting zoos" to try out new devices: 35% of Americans ages 16 and older would "very likely" use that service and another 34% say they would be "somewhat likely" to do so.

GPS-navigation apps to help patrons locate material inside library buildings: 34% of Americans ages 16 and older would "very likely" use that service and another 28% say they would be "somewhat likely" to do so.

"Redbox"-style lending machines or kiosks located throughout the community where people can check out books, movies or music without having to go to the library itself: 33% of Americans ages 16 and older would "very likely" use that service and another 30% say they would be "somewhat likely" to do so.

"Amazon"-style customized book/audio/video recommendation schemes that are based on patrons' prior library behavior: 29% of Americans ages 16 and older would "very likely" use that service and another 35% say they would be "somewhat likely" to do so.

When Pew Internet asked the library staff members in an online panel about these services, the three that were most popular were classes on e-borrowing, classes on how to use handheld reading devices, and online "ask a librarian" research services. Many librarians said that their libraries were already offering these resources in various forms, due to demand from their communities.

These are some of the key findings from a new national survey of 2,252 Americans ages 16 and older by the Pew Research Center's Internet & American Life Project and underwritten by a grant from the Bill & Melinda Gates Foundation. The interviews were conducted on October 15-November 10, 2012 and done on cell phone and landlines and in English and Spanish.

● Public priorities for libraries

Asked for readers or students thoughts on which services libraries should offer to the public, majorities of Americans are strongly in favor of:

Coordinating more closely with local schools: 85% of Americans ages 16 and older say libraries should "definitely" do this. Offering free literacy programs to help young children: 82% of Americans ages 16 and older say libraries should "definitely do" this. Having more comfortable spaces for reading, working, and relaxing: 59% of Americans ages 16 and older say libraries should "definitely do" this. Offering a broader selection of e-books: 53% of Americans ages 16 and older say libraries should "definitely do" this. These services were also most popular with the library staff members in our online panel, many of whom said that their library had either already implemented them or should "definitely" implement them in the future. At the same time, people have different views about whether libraries should move some printed books and stacks out of public locations to free up space for tech centers, reading rooms, meeting rooms, and cultural events: 20% of Americans ages 16 and older said libraries should "definitely" make those changes; 39% said libraries "maybe" should do that; and 36% said libraries should "definitely not" change by moving books out of public spaces.

Americans say libraries are important to their families and their communities, but often do not know all the services libraries offer. Fully 91% of Americans ages 16 and older say public libraries are important to their communities; and 76% say libraries are important to them and their families. And libraries are touchpoints in their communities for the vast majority of Americans: 84% of Americans ages 16 and older have been to a library or bookmobile at some point in their lives and 77% say they remember someone else in their family using public libraries as they were growing up. Still, just 22% say that they know all or most of the services their libraries offer now. Another 46% say they know some of what their libraries offer and 31% said they know not much or nothing at all of what their libraries offer.

● Changes in library use in recent years

In the past 12 months, 53% of Americans ages 16 and older visited a library or bookmobile; 25% visited a library website; and 13% used a handheld device such as a smartphone or tablet computer to access a library website. All told, 59% of Americans ages 16 and older had at least one of those kinds of interactions with their public library in the past 12 months. Throughout this report we call them "recent library users" and some of our analysis is based on what they do at libraries and library websites. Overall, 52% of recent library users say their use of the library in the past five years has not changed to any great extent. At the same time, 26% of recent library users say their library use has increased and 22% say their use has decreased. The table below highlights their answers about why their library use changed:

● How people use libraries

Of the 53% of Americans who visited a library or bookmobile in person in the past 12 months, here are the activities they say they do at the library:

73% of library patrons in the past 12 months say they visit to browse the shelves for books or media.

73% say they visit to borrow print books.

54% say they visit to research topics that interest them.

50% say they visit to get help from a librarian. Asked how often they get help from library staff in such things as answering research questions, 31% of library patrons in the past 12 months say they frequently get help, 39% say they sometimes get help, 23% say they hardly ever get help, and 7% say they never get help.

49% say they visit to sit, read, and study, or watch or listen to media.

46% say they visit to use a research database.

41% say they visit to attend or bring a younger person to a class, program, or event designed for children or teens.

40% say they visit to borrow a DVD or videotape of a movie or TV show.

31% say they visit to read or check out printed magazines or newspapers.

23% say they visit to attend a meeting of a group to which they belong.

21% say they visit to attend a class, program, or lecture for adults.

17% say they visit to borrow or download an audio book.

16% say they visit to borrow a music CD.

These survey indicated that African-Americans and Hispanics are more likely to say libraries are important to them and their families, to say libraries are important to their communities, to access the internet at the library (and feel internet access is a very important service libraries provide), to use library internet access to hunt/apply for jobs, and to visit libraries just to sit and read or study. For almost all of the library resources we asked about, African-Americans and Hispanics are significantly more likely than whites to consider them "very important" to the community. That includes: reference librarians, free access to computers/internet, quiet study spaces, research resources, jobs and careers resources, free events, and free meeting spaces.

When it comes to future services, African-Americans and Hispanics are more likely than whites to support segregating library spaces for different services, having more comfortable spaces for reading, working and relaxing, offering more learning experiences similar to museum exhibits, helping users digitize material such as family photos or historical documents. Also, minorities are more likely than whites to say they would use these new services specified in the charts below.

Statistical analysis that controls for a variety of demographic factors such as income, educational attainment, and age shows that race and ethnicity are significant independent predictors of people's attitudes about the role of libraries in communities, about current library services, and about their likely use of the future library services we queried. In addition, African-Americans are more likely than whites to say they have "very positive" experiences at libraries, to visit libraries to get help from a librarian, to bring children or grandchildren to library programs.

● Second hand book market

Why is used car market similar to second hand car market consumer behavior ? When one publish decides to sell one used book. It will concern that how much the used book sale price and it won't need to concern the author can receive any royalties and have no economic interest in the text – when you buy the text, not a single penny goes to me. It's designed to be a "disposable," one-use text in order to keep the price down. (The used book market actually drives up the price of texts – to see why, think of what would happen to car prices if used car sales were not permitted.) How does the used car markets drive up the price of the good? With an used market, the buyer is willing to pay more, knowing that he can resell later. However, without an used market, everyone is forced to buy new cars, raising demand, and thus raising the price of new cars. How to think about these countervailing effects? It seems that second had book and car markets , they have similar characteristics to influence consumer behaviors.

Are the used books and used cars market actually analogous like the professor suggests? The professor and his publisher have a monopoly on the new textbook, but no one controls the new car market. Therefore, if people keep reselling text, the publisher will use their monopoly and raise the price of new books to compensate. In contrast, car manufacturers can't do so due to competitive pressure.Imagine that there are two kinds of people, rich and poor, and no market for used books. Rich people are willing to pay more for new textbooks. Poor people cannot afford to buy new textbooks. In the absence of a market for used books, poor people will not buy textbooks.

Imagine now that there is market for used books. Poor people are now able and willing to pay second hand textbooks. And rich people now have someone to sell the books too once they are done using these books. A market for second hand textbooks raises the price of textbooks because some people are not able and willing to buy new textbooks but are willing to buy second hand textbooks. In the absence of such a market, they'll spend their income on other goods that they deem more important.

Think of it otherwise this way. In the absence of a market for used textbooks the full value of a textbook is not exploited because some people who would wish to trade with one another cannot trade with one another. From what I can understand, in the context of the used books market, lets assume that there is set, finite amount of demand for the books. When there is a used books market, the demand first goes to the used books market and finishes up the supply in that market. The remaining demand then goes to the new books market (the professor/publisher). To compensate for the loss in demand, the publisher would therefore have to raise prices of the new books.

Now for the cars market, when there is no used cars market, everyone is indeed forced to buy new cars which raises demand and consequently price. However, you are assuming that cars are a necessity and that the demand transfers 100% from used cars to new cars. Some people maybe only purchasing cars from used cars market because they see the value in the lower price. When there is no longer a used car market, if the price of the new car remains the same, then people would deem that price to be too expensive since they are unable to resell it later on and ultimately choose not to buy at all or opt for alternatives. This actually reduces demand. To capture the market of such consumers, the car companies would ultimately reduce prices to get the market share. This is from the Bertrand competition model point of view.

● Is It Best to Buy or Borrow Books?

In gneral, reader will choose either to visit library to borrow books or visit book shop to buy book. In any readers' reading behavioral choice process, they will compare whether the book shop has same book to sell or library has same book to borrow, if the book can be sold or borrowed in shop or library. Then, the reader will compare the price between the library's the book list price and the shop's the book sale price. Hence, if the library's the book list price is more expensive to compare the shop's same book's sale price. Then, the reader will choose to visit the book shop to buy the same book in possible. So, his earlier borrowing the book desire will be changed to visit the book shop to buy the same book because the book shop's same book's sale price is cheaper than the library's same book. Unless, the reader does not visit the book shop , so he believes that the library's the book can not be sold from any book shops.

One major positive of buying books is more money in the pockets of authors, who — unless they're someone like Harry Potter creator J.K. Rowling — tend to need all the sales they can get. Plus you're giving business to bookstores. Then there's the pleasure of adding another title to your home shelves — where the book is always available for reading, for impressing guests with your superior taste in literature.

But taking out titles from your local library has advantages, too. It's free — an especially nice price in these grim economic times. It's eco-friendly, because many people eventually peruse the same copy. And it can lead to more reading, because there's a deadline for when the books need to be returned. Sure, you can renew a book. But I try to avoid that. If I borrowed four library books the month before, I'll stay up late a few nights before the due date to finish that last one. I read approximately 10 more novels a year that way. Last but not least, library users are supporting an important government institution at a time when many right-wingers want to close or privatize almost everything that's not making a profit for greedy corporations. America needs democratic places that welcome everyone, not just people with lots of money.

I first came across this comparison on a popular sales psychology website [link below], and it got me thinking... how do these kind of (genius) persuasion techniques apply to your career as an author? You see, whatever people might say, books – especially ebooks – are cheap. Most self-publishers who sell books on Kindle (or wherever) set the bar at $2.99 – $5.99 per title. And I just know you break out in nervous sweats at the thought of charging more than that. I know I do. But price isn't the only thing readers care about. In many cases, it isn't even their top priority. Raise your hand – ever dropped your book prices down to 99c in the hopes of picking up some much-needed sales? I know I have. But the main problem isn't to do with price. $2.99 or $3.99 or $5.99 isn't a lot of money. It just isn't. The problem is all about POSITIONING.

Car market is similar to book market. In car market, that is, making your prices seem like a good deal. And that's where your sales message comes in. In the case of the car advertisements above – the sales messages focus on what's important to the prospective buyer and frame it as a benefit. The Rolls-Royce drivers want opulence and calm. The Land Rover crowd want power and ruggedness (which they associate with a noisy engine).

In education and car markets, Think about it like this – millions of people spend $50,000 – $100,000 on a college education. Or $30,000 on a new car. Or $500 on marketing and advertising for their business. Or $200 on a new cover design for their book (you can substitute your own numbers – but you get the idea). And this doesn't feel like a bad deal. Because you're getting what you expect at the price you expect to pay for it. You trust the person or business selling to you. It feels like a good deal, and you're more than happy to pay.

Which brings me to my main point. There are three types of reader in this world:

– First, those who will buy ANYTHING you publish without even thinking twice.

– Second, those who will NEVER buy from you.

– Third, those who aren't ready to buy... yet.

Hence, any paper book shops or publishers need to consider that they must have ebook publishers and libraries to be their competitors. Any readers can choose to go to libraries to borrow to read or pay visa to buy the epublisher's ebooks to read from internet. So, technology had influences any readers' reading habits to change from traditional paper book reading method to ebook reading method. Technology factor will influence readers or book buyers their reading behavioral change. So, any authors' paper books prices can not be raised rapidly , even their prices can not charge more than ebook prices. Otherwise, readers or paper book buyers can choose to read any ebooks to replace paper books from internet channel. Because ebook publishers have more effort to replace any paper book publishers, when paper book readers are influenced to accept to apply internet channel to read any ebooks in popular. So, traditional paper book publishing will change to ebook publishing market in the future.

● Online vs offline book shop different development trend

Nowadays, online book publishing is one kind of popular sale method to global publishing. For example, Amazon publish is as a business model with many potential advantages, relative to a physical operation. It held out the potential of lower book inventing and distribution costs and reduced overhead. Consumers could find the books, they were looking for more easily and a variety book topic choices could be offered for sale. It can accept and fulfill orders from almost any domestic location with equal ease. And most purchasers made on its site would be exempt from sales tax. One Amazon strategy hand, it would have to make its returns and redress processes transparent and reliable, and offer other ways for clients to learn, as much about the book possible before buying. Future online book market development trend, such as Amazon, Barnes & Noble etc. online book shops. How closely would their clietns find book ordering, as a substitute for visiting book stores?

In fact, Amazon is global the largest ingle online booksellers and sells many other products. Otherwise, Barnes & Noble, have been market share diminsh obviously. In the future, Noble & Barnes both will have their market share diminish continue obviously. There are also many fewer specialty re lowest. Hence, it seems online and offline both publishing methods will be competitive. It brings this questions: What is the trend between online book sale channel, its size relative to offline book sales channel, growth rate and the charcteristcs of reders who by online in the future? How book market's online channels are economically different , due to e-commerce's effects on online book market and supply fundamentals? How an online book sales channel might be expected to change equilibrium market outcomes?

I believe online book channel based sale activity varies considerably on these aspects: Sales in manufacturing printing cost, online sale services and online demand print book sale book topic choices. Such as author online advertising, change more or less sale price, online paper book shippng cost, visa card discount or online book shop member card discount book purchase, what welfares to online book buyers are.

Why readers chooce to buy books from internet habitally? In tradition, online book buyers habitally hope to use the internet to buy. Generally, they have these characteristics: They hope to use the internet to buy electronic books at home, they enjoy to read electronic book from computer, it is in any regular capacity , not ncecessarily to visit book shops to find books to buy and they can search any electronic from internet, electronic book is convenient to read from computer or laptop when they catch transportation or going to anywhere. Usually, internet users are higher income, more educated and younger. It seems that education is a sizeable determinant of who is online, even controlling for income. However, gender does not seems to be a factor in explaining internet use. Moreover, many of book qualitative patterns are seen for online book purchases in general are observed for electronic book products on on demand printing book products in particular.

Predition in future, many of the traditional online products , such as electronic or print on demand books, computer hardware , electronic airline tickets, saw more modest , but still substantial growth. In the future, online sellers trend to be newer online book stores and have less brand or reputation capital to signal or famous brand quality. These factors can create in online book sellers, which also often involve delay. However, there are many reasons for online book purchasing. The most obvious is that readers don't have opportunity where unobservably inferior point of electronic or demand on print book purchases.

● Pricing strategy in online and offline
book retailing

The book price represents consumer behavior on price. On one hand, the model contains two probability fuctions which render consumers' reservation prices for each individual channel. On the other hand, it is based on numerous book distribution which represent probabilities from and to each online or offline book store separate channel. Price strategy of book sale concerns how readers select a particualr book? Both offine and online book information seeking price strategies point out the challenges for information systems development. Hence, book price decision based on readers' age, e.g. children book price will be chealer than adult book price, due to children book content is usually simple and papers page is less. Otherwise, adult book content is more complicated or difficult to understand and page number is more than children book page number. However, online book store disadvantages are that : information system still often fail in supporting the users in causal leisure situations. In order to improve online book search system. Online book stores need to be better understood user strategies and performance and translate them into purposeful features.

A common analysis approach is to compare price and user strategies and interactions in the digital environment with those that occue in similar physical environment. If online bookstores hope to decide more reasonable electronic books or on demand printing books sale prices to compete with offline bookstores. Since, the physical environment ( in this particular case bookstores) usually preceds the development of digital environments, processes and strategies from interaction in the physical environment have already stabilized and experiences can be translated into patterns for digital information system development. Thus, some only digital electronic bookstores , such as Amazon publish' disadvantages are : It lacks physical bookstore environment sale experiences. Otherwise, some owning themselves physical book and online book sale environment bookstores, bookstores that can compare only either paper books or electronic books bookstores to predict what the reasonable sale book sale price more easily. Are these differencs between online/digital book discovery environments and offline ( neighborhood bookstore) services? Are researching recommendation strategies differences between observable in online and offline book search sessions? In general, interactive users studies based on user interactions in a ISBS developed web-based book discovery information system are aggregated cross multiple researcher groups. In order to provide a realistic book discovery environment, book collection should be large and comparable to other book discovery systems ,such as online book sale. For example, Amazon library book collection is used consisting of approximately 1.5 million books. Each book contains general metadata ( title, authors, publisher, publication , year, etc. ) subject metadata ( classification, code), subject headings , user generated content ( Amazon publish user reviewer, library thing user tags).

How does India book market trend?

Thus, I believe that online or offline bookstore different book research method will also influence readers' preferable book choices, then their choices behavior will influence how many times to find the book easily. If the online or offline readers can find the book topic or author name or contents etc. information easily. Then, the sale chance of the book will increase. Thus, price can increase more. For high population country, e.g. India, China . Does it have more sale chance, due to many people are living in these countries? What us online book store trend in India? Online book can let readers to buy new books and old books from internet, rent or borrow books from internet or access it in the form of e book, e.g. Amazon publish is the big player of online book business in India today. India where dynamic technologies like mobiles are prevalent, e-book readers may soon make into average household. Some of publishing houses which predicted that it would be long journey for e –books to become part of life needs to India readers. Thus, India will be one potential e book market. India is the third biggest market for English books. However, there are challenges of online bookstore in India. IN fact, online book market has changed the way reading consumer use internet for knowledge. Nowadays, people prefer e books are accessible anywhere, any time for creating flexible and secure online bookstore for online bookstores that need to concern to sell their e books to India markets because India readers shall concern visa card payment method where it is safe to pay to read any e books from internet.

Besides, online information searching has touched every field of human life. In the future, it is possible that purchased via mobile are clothing/footwear and e book or on demand print books. Also , due to e book is one kind of popular reading product to be enter India market. Currently, the online book market in India is offering exciting and renewed services to the internet users. India readers can accept to buy old books to read from online sale channel. Thus, India will be one new second hand online book store market to follow developed countries, such as US, UK etc.

Trend and development in the global book market

Under the influence of internet, new media , social networks. The way in which search to satisfy our needs. Internet is the high technological search method to change at the level of products and services, such as e book ( electronic book or demand on print electronic paper book) and online e book rent service , online library e book borrowing services. Thus, in the future, global book market will be popular on concentrating selling e books or online print on demand paper books more than general walk in offline book shop paper books sale only method. Due to, internet changes traditional readers' reading habits to enjoy to read e books from mobiles, laptops, desktops more than paper book reading. Thus, the global book market will be predicted online electronic book sale format more than visiting walk in book ship sale format. The digitalization of information enables us to bring into discussion today contents separated from the physical, materials, paper shapes of the book. Today, books could be found online, read online for free or downloaded as an e book in English or any other language. Practically, the book has changed from paper to electronic book. In until , the internet and the e book , the changes were extremely slow. Today, digitalization produces rapid changes to the entire system of printing, distribution and reading books. Hence, the global book market trend will be the major implication on publishes, distribution, authors and book consumers. The online competition brings major changes to traditional distributors, the bookstores, the author of independent distributors noticeable decreased. The number of big distributors' stores will decrease. For example, Amazon publish is the best known global selling books online. Although, it can sell e books and printing on demand paper books both from internet channel conveniently.

In conclusion, e book market will dominate global online electronic book sale market and the e book publisher number will increase. As the same time, the visiting walk in offline book shop number will decrease, due to readers have accept to use laptops, mobiles to read electronic books from internet channel more than reading paper books. It implies paper book publishers need to change sale method, e.g. adopting internet to sell print on demand paper books, or reducing paper book sale price to attract e book readers to choose to buy paper books to read.

Web vs School campus book store development trend

Why do students choose to buy textbooks online? What factors motivate students choose online textbooks purchase? Nowadays, many online book retailers, such as Varsity books.com and Bigword.com ,. Amazon publish.com are now capturing more of the textbook online store market. What is motivating this behavior changes to student market , instead of children story market, entertainment or travel or sport book market etc. topic market. What causes students to choose purchase textbooks online ? Can likelihood to make purchases online by predicted by various social and personal characteristics of consumers? The online textbook purchase growth is allowing online retailers to capture a substantial portion of sales in some sectors. What motivates consumers to shop on the web? But, what if these factors are nor significant , such as better product availability, lower cost, as is that case when comparing on offline textbook purchasing. There is no significant price advantage to buy textbook online, it is there an availability issue, given that textbook can be purchased in the campus store ( Foucault et al., 2000).

I shall assume that precious positive online purchase is positively correlated with the likelihood of an individual purchasing textbooks online. Hence, it influences why readers choose to buy textbooks online again. Following , other factor web consumers are likely shop online to save time and/or money, but what of those consumers who shop online when an equally time and cost efficient alternative is present. With regard to textbook purchasing, the time invested in researching for the appropriate books is likely to be similar, regardless of whether the student bookstore or through an online textbook. With regard to textbook purchasing, the time invested in researching from the time invested in searching appropriate books is likely to be similar: regardless of whether the student chooses to shop in the campus bookstore or through an online textbook retailer. If time from purchase until use counts, online textbook shopping could be considered less time efficient than its offline counterpart. Due to the readers need to turn on computer to link to internet to read electronic books or wait the print on demand to buy paper books from the electronic book store web site to wait the paper books to post to the online book buyer's home. Otherwise, offline bookstores can reduce time spending to wait the books to be posted to the buyer's home, after who pay money to take the paper book from the bookstore immediately. So, the non-waiting post book issue is still the text bookstore's strength to attract students to buy.

Prediction of direction of electronic books future trend

What is future trend of electronic book publishing development? To answer this question, we need to know what benefits of ( electronic books) can attribute to human's needs. Nowadays, electronic books ( e-books) are one way to enhance the digital library with global 24 hours a day and 7 days a week access to authoritative information, and there enable users to quickly retrieve and access specific research materials easily, quickly and effectively. Evenm some ebooks publishers choose to let readers who can borrow ebooks to online readers to read from online libraries to earn profit. For example, Amazon publisher lets every Amazon readers only pay about US$5 per month. Then, who can borrow unlimited ebooks to read from Amazon publisher private online member library website convenently.

Thus, it is one ebooks online borrowing strategy to compette with offline book stores and public library and school library in publishing industry. Due to offline book stores lack borrowing books services to any walk in readers. However, some countries' publich libraries also have similar ebooks borrowing to read services. An an ebook providers' electonic online libraries, online computer library center has been involved in the selection, catalogue and distribution of ebooks. Library users can able to remotely search, locate and checkout ebooks from the library's online public access catalogues. Thus, ebook publisher will have another public library competitor which can provide similar ebook borrowing service to online ebook readers from public library websites.

It means ebook publishers need to adopt any attractive ebook library sale borrowing service strategy to attract public library readers. However, as with any new opportunity, new challenge utilizes the internet opportunity to deliver new book content is no exception, Integrating ebooks into the digital library has created challenges and opportunities for librarians, publishers and ebooks providers for librarians in this ebook library borrowing service market to earn extra ebook lending service income. Because, online borrowing service library can have ebooks borrowing service, then why online ebook readers need to choose independent ebook publisher individual borrowing book service website to replace traditional public library paper book borrowing service. The reasons possible include that the readers can borrow ebooks to study from ebook publisher individual library borrowing website at home conveniently, but it is possible that they can not find any paper books to borrow from public libraries which are the same ebooks to be borrowed from any one ebook store to read, also ebook publishers can let whose ebook borrowers to borrow unlimited ebooks to read and there are longer extend borrowing ebook return days more than public libraries borrowing book return days and ebook readers have no penalty when they return ebooks too late and they can choose to pay little borrowing ebook charge in the month, if who do not expect to borrow any ebooks in the month, who can choose to stop to pay borrowing ebook charge in the month. Hence, they can choose to continue to borrow unlimited ebook numbers from ebook publishers and they are permitted to return ebooks longer time to compare traditional public libraries. For example, when the ebook reader pay only US$5 ebook library service fee to the ebook publisher in the month , then who can borrow the number of ebook up to 50 maximum number in the month as well as who can return the all ebooks to the ebook library within 60 days, it is longer return days to compare traditional public libraries. If the ebook reader can not return all these ebooks after the return day of 60 day. They can permit to extend more 60 return days. After this another 60 return days, they only need to pay US$5 penalty to the ebook store. Thus, it is one attrative ebook library borrowing service strategy in this competitive book publishing industry.

There is no doubt that the same trends that adopts ebooks and e-readers to US ebook publishing market are having a similar effect in other countries as well, such as Mobile ebook or laptop ebook technical development of reading devices that provide an reading experience similar to that of reading an actual book, the increasing penetration of the internet in all areas of life, which is significantly changing reading patterns and reading behavior. The increasing extent to which ebook or demand on printing book consumers are open to new technological reading trends, for which in particular that availability of attractive mobile devices, such as smartphones, portable games consoles, and MPS players are responsible to ebook reader tools.

Future trend will be that publishers and authors need to build close digital cooperation relationship. Publishers, bookstores and device manufacturers should take the opportunity to provide the market now with innovative ebook publishing products. And authors should explore opportunities for digital distributions and support publishers in their efforts to publish content. Publishers should also design a giving strategy and attractive ebook sale website that attracts customers without undermining the value of content. A well-thought out pricing strategy may also help publishers and content gain new customers, those who would not have purchased a traditional book , but may be inclined to buy an ebook that costs less, offers additional features , and works on a digital device . They already own there, usually the ebook price compares to traditional paper book price which have similar content, ebook price will be cheaper them the similar content of traditional paper book sale price.

In the future, ebook publishers will need to position themselves as content providers, and not just the suppliers of physical books. They will have to make content available on multiples media, in multiple formats, on multiple platforms. This content may not be limited to the text of a book itself, it may also include videos and games. This additional content may lead to incremental revenue.

In fact, the only lesisure activities more popular than reading books were watching television, listening to music such the radio and reading newspapers and magazines. Thus, every one should need to choose to enjoy to do what kinds of leisure activities every day. For example, if one person chooses to spend much time to either watch television or listen the music and radio or read newspapers and magazines in the whole day. I believe that he will spend less time to read book in the day. Then, it implies that ebook or paper book readers , the paper book or ebook buyer number will be decrease, due to they spend less time to read or without any reading behavior in the day. Thus, how to persuade every one to feel that reading book habit is attractive or important which can be one factor to influence the paper or electronic book readers, even electronic or paper book buyer number. Thus issue will be an attractive topic to concern for every ebook or paper book publisher on book publishing industry. If these both kind of publishers can persuade any person to feel reading book habit can bring benefits to themselves. They will spend less time to leisure activities. Then, ebook or paper book sale number or ebook borrowing service income will raise in the future. Thus, these both kinds of publishers need to concern how to persuade people to choose to spend some time to read books habitually every day. Consequently, psychological factor will be one important direction to raise book buyer number in publishing industry.

What are the factors to influence sales and marketing strategies for publishers?

I feel that how to predict book buyers which is driven by book buying experience and the publisher's credibility ( loyalty) factors which will influence the any book buyer whose make final decision to buy the book from the publisher. As a publisher, a major goal is to extend whose readership and extend whose readers' influences, but where to start? How do publishers understand and serve diverse readers and decision makers in different countries? Whether can readers find the kind topic of book from publishers only, when find the kind topic of book from the university libraries or public libraries? Hence, due to offline and online publishing industry competition is high, global publishers will need to develop a sales plan to satisfy readers' reading taste. For publishers need to conduct book exhibition activities, visit different author's decision makers to research what who like to write negotiate terms to publish books with individual authors, secure sales and manage orders etc. different regulations of publishing to every author.

I recommend online or offline publisher ought concern how to publish every book before they decide to sel their every electronic book or paper book to any countries' readers. The marketing strategy includes to develop plan every book sale projection, SWOT ( strengths, weaknesses, opportunities, or threats ) to every book to be published to the country's readers to implement the plan. Book sales program, email communication marketing, lead generation to analyze the results, eg. every book purchasing trends, customer profiles, marketing sementation for every book to follow up and bedrief: Measuring ROI, setting priorities and develops tastics, finally customer needs analysis foe every book sale, it includes GAP analysis, ebook online library visits numbers to experience the ebook and focus groups. The, it is cycle to the develop plan again. Thus, if the publisher can have a better understanding of pricing strategy plan which can create price plan to be strengthed changes or cancelled for every paper book or electronic book sale marketing price strategies. Bringing potentially and disastrous reading experience to readers , this factor can be one good method to increase reader number and book sale price and sale number method. Then, the ebook or paper book publishers can make more accurate ebook or paper book sale price to every sale market, e.g. US or UK which is better book sale market, which kind of book can be the popular to these either market, whether UK readers like to read ebooks more or US readers like to read ebooks more or US readers like to read paper books more or UK readers like to read paper books more. Thus, the ebook or paper book stores can gather these data to analyze whether what every book topic sale price is more accurate to achieve the highest sale number and income.

Consequently, more appealing offerings can be developed to broader every publisher's audience and enhanced whose every publisher's image, segments of reader research, e.g. reader age, book reading taste. This is a measure level of penetration of journals and identity opportunity for growth GAP analysis marketing strategies will be popular methods to future book publishing. Based on first hand, expensive visiting and surveying librarians around the world, examing factors unique to each country and culture and make to recommendations integrate in every publisher's communication plan. For example, ebook trends pecentage of ebok spending in online ebook borrowing libraries is a publishing extra income from ebook borrowing readers. It is such one part of the overall electronic book market share income in the electronic book publishing market. In conclusion, internet technological innovation can bring new publishing business chance to ebook development , but it also brings competition to traditional paper book stores. So, paper book stores need have good marketing strategies to win their new ebook competitors.

Analysis of factors influencing online newspaper reading behavior
Nowadays, online newspapers will be popular to let readers to read any newspapers' news from internet. It showed that for online newspapers reader's intention is influenced by performance expectancy, habit and the habit of reading a print newspapers. So, newspapers consumer personal reading behavior was influenced by intention and habit. Some reading behavioral researchers showed some reasons to explain why traditional paper newspaper readers will like to change habits to study online newspapers.

Hence, changing reading habit will be one factor to influence traditional paper newspaper reader individual reading behavior changes to online newspapers reading habit. In fact, high technological communication media will influence mobile phone and internet both new communication media causes. These new communication medias will bring new print electronic media causes, such as print newspapers, online book products. Some of traditional paper newspaper readers will choose to read any news from online newspapers. The reasons include free charge, reading at home in convenient, not need go out newspapers, online newspapers do not need the reader's hands to touch the black word paper newspaper to be dirty, and waste less time to buy every day to achieve economic benefit.

Every online newspaper reader will have this factor to influence whom to change traditional paper newspaper reading habit. The factor shows that attitude has a direct effect on intentions, and is influenced by performance expectancy and effort expectancy or related personal online reading acceptance conceptions. Because of whose acceptance of online newspaper reading attitude is as an important in technology user online newspaper reading attitude was included.

Additional, every online newspaper reader self-efficacy and anxiety are expected to be minor issue to influence the online newspaper reader to change whose attitude to choose not to internet tool to read of an online newspaper. However, different age reader either he/she is young or old age factor will have influence whom to choose online newspaper to read, e.g. old age readers will feel difficult to apply internet technology to read newspaper, otherwise, young age readers will feel easy to apply internet technology to read newspaper. So, the old or young age traditional paper newspaper readers, when the acceptance new technological online newspaper to them, they will adopt online newspaper reading attitude to replace traditional paper newspaper reading habit more easy. So, their acceptance new technological of online newspaper reading attitude will have a direct effect on online newspaper reading intention and are influenced by both paper and online newspapers reading enjoyment performance expectation and online newspapers reading effort expectation, when their expectations were needed to be satisfied more these past traditional paper newspaper reading experience. Moreover, past paper newspapers reading behavior and habit should be noted. Then, these two expectation factors will encourage or persuade the traditional paper newspaper readers change whose reading attitude, reading habit and reading behavior to read online newspapers. Hence, the online newspaper readers' psychological factor will influence whose traditional paper newspapers readers whose reading behavioral changes. Also, it means that expectation factor will influence the traditional newspaper readers to change whose counter intentional paper newspaper reading habit.

However, online newspaper will bring much knowledge to compare traditional paper newspapers , e.g. real newspapers news data, more meaningfulness news, providing the nature of visiting a news website, which can let online news readers can feel different read model primary on frequency with relatively little spread in the amounts of time spent at the site.

What are the main factors to influence online newspaper reading behaviors? Same testing indicates for moderation by the online newspaper age, gender and online newspaper reading experience will bring the online reading newspapers habit influence. The testing also indicates male gender and young age group , this group likes to apply internet to find or seek or search any news matters. Hence, this internet user group will bring to have interest to read newspapers from internet channel. The reason is possible because this young male internet users like to contact new technology, e.g. internet. They think the online newspaper is useful and it is more useful to read the online newspaper to compare to paper newspaper.

The two reasons : liking to contact new technology and feeling the online newspaper is more useful which can support why young male online internet users feel to expect reading online newspaper expectancy were more concrete.

Additional online newspapers usefulness are more considered on unclear concept to explain why this reader group feels more like to study online newspapers. What exactly is the usefulness of reading an online newspaper?

The testing also indicated that some online newspaper readers responded to use the online newspaper to feel natural, it showed to be related to attitude as well as to habit , which seems to hold face validity as a natural feel can be considered on attitude on the online newspaper. So, online reading attitude and online reading habit can reflect why man young male like to read online newspapers more than paper newspaper reason.

Another reason indicated that when the young male readers want to read the news, the online newspaper is an obvious choice for him/her. So, many online newspaper young male readers had felt online newspaper is one another newspaper reading choice to replace traditional paper newspapers.

In conclusion , free charge online newspaper is not the main factor to influence both traditional paper newspaper readers to change their reading habit to choose online newspapers to read suddenly. There are other factors to cause them to choose online newspapers to read, such as more usefulness feeling, contacting new technology, online reading habit, positive online reading attitude etc. different psychological factors which will have more influences to cause their paper newspaper reading habits to be changed. Hence, the free price economic gain actor must not only one main factor to persuade readers to choose online newspapers to read.

How electronic versus traditional print
textbook influence of university students'
learning behavior

When one university student was accepted by electronic text book learning channel to replace traditional paper text book learning channel ( methods). Electronic text book will bring what positive or/and negative influence to impact whose learning behavior changes. For example, electronic text book learning method will bring positive impact to raise the student's examination grades and perceived learning scores or it will bring negative impact to fall down the student's examination grades and perceived learning scores. The mean scores indicated that students who choose to text books for their learning aim. It will have significantly higher perceived affective learning performance and examination results. Thus, the purpose of student learning and teacher teaching method, every university needs to examine whether it is efficient to raise student learning effort to replace paper text book learning method in any learning environment, e.g. many students and one teacher classroom learning environment or the independent student learns himself/herself at home learning environment or library learning environment.

Can text book reading tool bring absolute advantages to university students or bring some disadvantages to them? When a student needs to apply e-text book to learn, who needs access e-text book in a static location, such as a computer or on a mobile device. So, the e-text book in a static location factor, it will have influence to each student reading or learning behavior to bring negative and/or positive both impacts.

The e-text book was distributed on a CD and installed on a located computer. This limited the user to accessing the e-textbook in a single location and eliminated the potential access to the e-text book on due to the lack of mobility. So, it seems that the location of limited to e-text book will bring negative impact to let the student can only learn in a fixed location because he/she will feel difficult to move heavy computer to other places to learn more than on paper text book. So, e-text book location can not allow the student to leave the classroom to learn more easier if he/she had chose to use to computer to install the CD to learn in the classroom. Supposing the student 's teacher needs the student often to leave the classroom to discuss any matter suddenly, it is not very convenient to the student to use e-text book to learn because he/she can not move the computer to leave the classroom with him/her easily. Then, it will be possible to influence the student can bot be attention to read the e-text book, when the teacher needs the student to leave the classroom ( none book bringing ) to discuss any time any time immediately. Otherwise, if the student used one paper book to read/learn in the classroom, if the teacher needs whom to leave the classroom often to discuss immediately. He/she will feel convenient to learn because he/she can bring the light paper book to leave the classroom to discuss with the teacher in any location easily.

Hence, it seems e-text book learning will bring not convenient fixed location learning environment to every e-texting learning student in classroom, when, he/she needs often to leave the classroom to discuss with the teacher any time.

Other disadvantage of e-text learning will bring students feel difficult in possible. In the past, some learning researcher experiments indicated results demonstrated that student participants in both groups had similar recall and ability to reinterpret information suggesting that retrieval of information is not effected by kindle e-book reader e-text book, a tabled computer e-text book or a print version.

Hence, it seems that e-text book can not help or assist recall the student's learning memory to remember the e-text book content more easier. Due to it is one e-text book machine, the student will fell to difficult to find any unclear or important information in any page(s) to write for learning/reading record more easier than one paper text book.

Another disadvantage of e-text book is the inefficacy or inefficient reading challenge to the e-text book reader. The efficacy of e-text books in a higher education environment will be one interesting discussing question. Passage length is one difference that impact the results. Studies involving shorter reading sessions indicated no substantial variance with respect to reading comprehension and understanding.

Conversely, studies involving longer reading passages indicated prior comprehension, when reading longer e-text , eye fatigue and mental workload are also concerns. Hence, e-text book reading will be possible to let students feel eye fatigue and mental workload in their reading process.

Due to machine e-text book words are more small size and unclear more than paper text book words to print to let students to read every words or sentences in computer. Consequently, studies indicated that e-text book readers need to spend much nervous and time to read longer and poor comprehension in whole e-text book reading process. When, university students need to spend time to read longer e-texts from computers. For example, they need to choose to reads hundreds of papers of e-text books on a screen, whether on a computer or handheld electronic device compared to print versions may contribute to eye fatigue. The consequence, eyestrain and mental fatigue could be poorer comprehension and have a poor eye, nervous health influence and every student's e-text learning behavior can bring negative reading habit to whom, when every one need to apply desktop or laptop or mobile electronic tools to read any words from e-textbooks. Hence, it seems e-text book reading method has possible to bring poor health challenge to every student.

So, above all these e-learning reading factors to bring this question: Does e-learning influence the student's negative reading behavior to cause poor final examination grades results? In fact, every student needs to change whose traditional learning method from paper text book reading habit or reading behavior to e-text books. He/she needs to change whose reading habit. He/she must need to spend long time to accept how to adopt this kind of new technological reading method as well as effect may change through a new technological learning experience itself and impacts the acquisition of knowledge leading to reading behavioral change.

As I indicated the e-learning will bring poor health and poor nervous negative influences when the student often needs to apply electronic product to read long time. So, it will be possible to influence the student health to be poor to bring examination low grades results in possible be cause he/she has poor health to exam.

It is possible that it has relationship to influence the student to exam low grade between e-learning habit and poor health causes. The reason is based on that efficacy of textbook format is defined grades. I assume that all these negative e-text book reading factors can influence every e-text book reader's health to be poor when he/she needs often read e-text book s to cause long time reading habit. So, I mean that e-text book reader individual health changes to poor, it is only depend on how long time e-text book reading habit factor. So, if he/she only spend less time to read e-text books and he/she also has habit to read paper books sometimes. Then, he/she won't be influenced to be poor from e-learning method easily.

It means that it has none direct relationship between less time e-text book reading habit and low examination grades result. Hence, low examination grades result to the student, it only depends on long time e-text book reading habit and the student's long time e-text book reading habit needs to confirm that whose long time e-text book reading habit causes poor health to the student effect. Why do I believe that efficacy of textbook format can influence the student's examination grade? Based on above analysis, the e-text book reading format and paper book reading format is very different. For example, the efficacy of textbook is very different between paper text book reading format and electronic text book reading format. Such as one sickness student needs to spend more nervous to read one e-text book more than one paper text book . This reason is because machine reading method is difficult to compare paper reading method. When the student has sickness, who must need to spend more time and nervous to read one e-text book more than one paper text book. If my assumption is right, then the e-text book sickness reader's reading efficacy to each paper must be poor to compare the paper text book sickness reader , due to the sickness e-text book reader needs to spend long time and much nervous to read each paper more than he/she chooses to read one paper book. When he/she is sickness to finish whose reading . Due to his/her memory will be poor and tries, when he/she feels sick, so whose reading effort must be poor when he/she needs to apply computer tools or mobiles to read.

How to change future e-reader study habit to feel better

Nowadays, publishers, internet bookstores manufacturer e-readers have high expectations for digital future of book industry. If they expected e-book publishing industry success, they need to considerate how to assist to future e-readers to let them to feel whose reading habit to be better in order to persuade or attract them to choose to read e-books more easily, due to doctors indicated that long time e-books reading will cause eye poor health and tired and poor nervous reason in possible and paper book price competition and more topic choice reason. It is one value consideration question that e-book publishers need to considerate.

For example, in the US Amazon publish has improved the reading market by producing e Reader that is easy to use and making it easy for clients to purchase a wide variety of books at competitive prices. It will bring digital reader technology as an opportunity to open new target markets and create new e-readers. The question is how Amazon publish , such as e-book publishers change future e-reader reading habit to feel to choose e-books reading method is better than paper books reading method. The successful factors may include as below:

E-book reading market is similar to e-music listening market. They need every e-book reader and/or digital music listen listener to discover why to apply this kind of new digital technology reading or listening method which is better to enjoy to read every e-book content and/or listen every digital music song in order to adopt new listening and/or reading digital technological learning habits or experiences. So, this new digital technological reading or/and digital music listening process, every e-book reader or digital music listener needs to learn how to adopt this kind new digital reading or/and listening products to change from his/her traditional paper book reading or/and CD/DVD music song listening method to this new technological digital reading or listening methods from computer tool channel.

In this changing habit process, every e-book reader or/and e-music listener needs to spend some time to learn how to apply internet technological tool to help whose to read digital book or listen digital music from computer channel. So, he/she must attempt to change whose habit from traditional paper book reading habit and/or CD/DVD listening music habit to e-book reading habit and/or e-music listening habit.

Furthermore, e-book publishers also need to know whether which kind of book topics are be favorable popular to be chose to read for either student reader target to read or mature age reader target to read or old age reader target to read. Who will purchase the topic to read to be e-Reader? Will they be designed to appeal to be a group of e-reader customers or only to those who have a high degree of comfort with technology to enjoy e-reading method? Will people who read once in a time be purchased by the small group of e-reading clients who buy and read a high volume of e-books? What reasons, readers will choose to read the topics of e-books more than paper books? Will publishers be able to use e-books and e-readers to extend the many different age e-reading clients, e.g. young, mature, retirement, old, student age e-readers? Will publishers ever more to all readers are only choose digital e-reading model habit or who are a half digital e-reader and a half paper book reading habit clients to them?

Hence, one successful digital publisher needs to consider how to persuade every traditional paper book habit readers to change their reading habit to read digital e-books from computer. Because changing habit is one challenge to influence the e-book publisher 's e-book reader number. How to persuade the paper book reading habit readers to change whose attitude to choose to read e-books , it is one considerate question to every digital publisher? Some readers may feel difficult that who needs to learn new knowledge how to read e-books from computer tool, e.g. old age reader group. This reason will influence they still choose paper books to read in habit. So, any e-book publisher has responsibility to teach new digital technological knowledge learning method to let the e-book desire readers can feel easy to apply internet to read e-books from computer tool.

Another factor is e-book price, normally every e-book price will need to be sold cheaper to compare the similar paper book topic in order to persuade paper book readers choose to buy the similar topic of e-books to read more easily. Because if the reader discover the e-book topic is similar to the paper book topic contents, but the e-book price is charged high than the similar paper book topic content, then he/she will possible to choose to buy the similar paper book topic to read.

Another factor concerns how to raise e-books attraction. E-publishers will need to position themselves as content providers, and not just to be similar to the suppliers of physical books. They will have to make content available on multiple media, in multiple formats, on multiple platforms. This content may not be limited to the text of a digital book itself, it may also include audio, video, image and sound speaking digital books to attract e-readers' attention.

Another factor is that I recommend e-book publishers need to let all e-book readers to feel reading e-books are leisure time habit to let them to enjoy life every day in popular. Intention is such as good tool for anyone to apply to entertainment, for example people linked using internet to read books, watch movies, play video games from computer tool. They are some main points. They have same main points. They tend to spend leisure time with electronic media, such as apply internet to watch television which is such as to apply internet one more choice to assist readers to read e-books from computer media tool conveniently at home.

However, this is one example e-book attraction point to e-reader. Every e-book needs have e-pub files to allow readers to control the size of the text or their computer screens. If the e-reader feels the text is small size and computer screen is small size in difficult to read. Then, he/she can use mouse tool to change the e-book text number to be high number, e.g. from 18 to 20 or more number and he/she can apply mouse tool to move the computer screen to be wider more easily. Hence, it is e-book attraction point to e-book readers to feel when he/she feel the text is small size to read in difficult. Otherwise, every paper book print text( word) size is fixed, all word size can not be changed to read and every paper book wide size is also fixed. All it is every paper's unattraction point to every paper book reader.

Consequently, every e-book publisher needs have its attraction point to let its every e-book reader feels it is different to the other paper book publishers. It needs to solve these challenges to let its every reader to accept to choose its e-book reading channel. The challenges may include how to let the e-reader feels its e-book reading media can provide a more comfortable e-reading experience to compare other e-book publishers' reading media, how to let its e-readers feels its all e-books can provide one precise and stable e-book reading characteristics, how to let its ebook readers to feel its every ebook displays does not require any background lighting and one easy to read, even in direct sunlight environment, and it e-reading tool can spend less energy from laptop battery or desktop electricity to compare other e-book publisher reading tool, it means that the e-book publisher's ebook reading tool can provide a recharged power desire which can be used for several thousand pages or seveal weeks e-reading function. Hence, it the e-book publisher's e-book reading tool can provide more clear words and text image as well as less electricity consumption function to let every e-reader to read to compare other ebook publishers from laptop, destop or mobile media. Then , the ebook publisher's competitive effort will raise to win its other ebook publishing competitors. However, any ebook publisher needs have attraction points to persuade its ebook readers to read its any ebooks feel comfortable and providing fun ebooks choices and easy to read its every ebook text more clear if it expects to win its competitors in ebook publishing industry.

Factors influence child reading habit

Reading failure is a serious educational problem to influence every publisher success because if the child chooses to buy its books to read, but its child readers can not feel its books can help them to assist their learning success or failure examination or low grades result. Then, it will influence its child reader number to be reduced. However, the factors cause reading failure, it is not only considered to the publisher's poor book content quality factor, it can include the other factors such as: It is simply be attributed by poverty, immigration or the learning of English as a second language. What factors will influence child read in wrong habit to bring reading failure, even learning failure in effect? It is one question to every publisher needs to know in order to avoid they feel failure examination emotion after read their e-text books. Hence, how to design every text book content is one important issue to ever publisher.

A study by Yankelovich found most children are reading, but they are not reading enough. It indicated only about 3 in 10 children can be classified as high frequency readers who read books for fun ever day. Age 8 children are less to see benefits t oreading for fun, girls are more likely boys to have positive attitude about reading and feel fun. The benefits of reading are evidenced by the attitude of high frequency readers to achieve future learng success. More than 40% of children ages 5 to 8 say they are high frequency readers, by ages 9 to 11 that proportation drops to 29%. Almost half of the 15 to 17 year old ( 46%) are low frequency readers compared with 14% of 5 to 8 year old age. So, this study investigation reflected that building good learning habit has relationship between frequency reading and feeling fun to read to every child. It seems that one fun content book can attract the child to read the whole book all content really. So, publisher needs to consider how to design and write attractive content books to let every child to read.

What factors cause every child feel barriers to read? Some investigations indicate that young children tend to maintain high expectations for success, even in the face of regarded failure, when old students don't, also to older students feel failure following high effort appears to carry more negative inplications. Moreover, all students individual attitude about their capabilities and their interpretation of success and failure is further factor to affect their willingness to feel fun to read in themselves learning proceses.

So, it concludes this fun book content design method can persuade young people feel fun to read really. Moviated readers hold positive benefits about themselves attitude or reading habit which will bring positive and attractive reading emotion to influence them.

What are the book publishers and teachers' responsibilities to improve student individual negative habit to have positive reading habit or positive learning attitude? The ultimate goal in teaching and reading book is to raise students comprehend te ideas in a piece of text as they need. So, any publisher has responsibility to publish one fun and meaning book in prior, because every teacher will teach whose students by the text book content. If the text book content is fun and attractive and meaning, then the teacher can teach to let every students to learn more easily.

Training every student owns good reading habit which can help whom expand their thinking skills, learn to concentrate and enlarge their vocabulary and effectively better their learning environment. The good reading habit ought be trained from the child stage in beginning. So, when the child has is growing up, when he/she is needed to go to primary, secondary, even university to study, he/she had been built good reading habit from the publishers' fun and meaning book content influence in order to let they further learn any new knowledge to feel more easily. So, publishers have responsibilities to sell fun and meaning content books to let every child to read to raise whom reading interest to further young and mature learning stages.

However, the problems, children experience learning to read are often not related to their ability to learn, but to their awareness. Their ability to hear the English language and their expose to the English words. So, repeating to spell the English words will assist the child to raise memory to remember to write the English words more easily. So, book publishers have responsibilities to express every book content to attact child readers to feel interest or fun to learn to remember to spell every word as well as teachers have responsibilities to train students how to hear the words, he/she assist every child to learn to spell the English word more easily. So, teachers ought often speak every word or speak every sentence loudly from every book content to let students to listen easily in order to let they can raise every word memory more easily.

Consequently, instead of child's parents and child himself/herslf has responsibility to help the child self to build good reading habit, teachers and book publishers have also responsibilities to help them to build good reading habit because fun and meaningful books which bring more attraction to influence every child to read, when the book is fun and meaningful , then the teacher can follow its content to teach whose students to attract them to learn more easily. However, the good reading habit includes elements of reading comprehension to every book content , such as: identifying and summarizing the main idea, comparing and contrasting, identifying supporting facts and details, making influences and drawing conclusions, predicting outcomes, recognizing fact and opinion, identigy cause and effect recognizing sequence of events, identifying story / case elemetnts, such as main characters, settings, conflict, and resolution, identifying the another's purpiose and point of view, interpreting literary devices, such as imagery , symbolisms.

Hence, publishers ought to follow above these elements to design their every book content in order to let child readers to feel fun and meaningful and easy to read. Because reading comprehension elements will be one important factor to train every child or mature student reader to build good reading habit or attitude more easily and effectively in order to raise their future good reading effort in their every learning stage in success.

# CHAPTER THREE

# Persuading space traveller leisure choice

The comparison benefit
and risk between space
travel and space exploration

When our money, time, technological resource, human resource is shortage, whether we ought concentrate on investing space travel entertainment and space exploration or choice of either one investment only. We need to evaluate whether future how much benefit we can earn more between either space travel and space exploration as well as whether what we will encounter more failure risk between space travel and space exploration. Hence, I feel that space scientists need to compare their benefit and risk both in order to concentrate on choosing only one implementation.

In prior , I shall indicate what the space exploration benefits and risks are. Latter I shall indicate what the space travel benefits and risks are. What does space exploration mean? Space exploration is the use of astronomy and space technology to explore outer space. physial exploration of space is conducted both by human spaceflights and by robotic spacecraft. There are different types of exploration? They may include:
•Arctic exploration •Cave exploration •Desert exploration •Mineral exploration •Ocean exploration •Space exploration •Urban exploration •Mountain exploration these different kinds of exploration. I feel space exploration will bring these possible benefits and risks as below:

On job creation aspect

The possible of space exploration may include as these: the popularly cited benefit of space exploration is "job creation", or the fact that a space agency and its network of contractors, universities and other entities help people stay employed. From time to time, NASA puts out figures concerning how many associated jobs a particular project generates, or the economic impact. Employment can also be full-time, part-time or occasional. So while "job creation" is cited as a benefit, more details about those jobs are needed to make an informed decision about how much good it does.

On education aspect

Teaching has a high priority for NASA, so much so that it has flown astronaut educators in space. (The first one, Christa McAuliffe, died aboard the space shuttle Challenger during launch in 1986. Her backup, Barbara Morgan, was selected as an educator/mission specialist in 1998 and flew aboard STS-118 in 2007.) And to this day, astronauts regularly do in-flight conferences with students from space, ostensibly to inspire them to pursue careers in the field. NASA's education office has three goals: making the workforce stronger, encouraging students to pursue STEM careers (science, technology, engineering and mathematics), and "engaging Americans in NASA's mission." Other space agencies also have education components to assist with requirements in their own countries. It's also fair to say the public affairs office for NASA and other agencies play roles in education, although they also talk about topics such as missions in progress.

On intangible benefits aspect

Added to this host of business-like benefits, of course, are the intangibles. What sort of value can you place on better understanding the universe? Think of finding methane on Mars, or discovering an exoplanet, or constructing the International Space Station to do long-term exploration studies. Each has a cost associated with it, but with each also comes a smidgeon of knowledge we can add to the encyclopedia of the human race. Space can also inspire art, which is something seen heavily in 2014 following the arrival of the European Space Agency Rosetta mission at Comet 67P/Churyumov–Gerasimenko. It inspired songs, short videos and many other works of art.

Instead of tangible and intangible aspects, space exploration may also include these advantages as below:

1. Space exploration allows us to prepare for potential hazards.

The universe is a vast place where hidden dangers could be lurking almost anywhere. Even if you consider only our solar system, there are asteroid and comet threats which could devastate our planet if an impact were to occur. Exploring space gives us an opportunity to locate these hazards in advance to prepare an encounter that could help to preserve our race. Then there are the interstellar items to consider. Oumuamua, or 11/2018 U1, was discovered by the Pan-STARRS1 telescope in 2017 by the University of Hawaii through funding from the Near-Earth Object Observations Program. It was originally thought to be an asteroid, then a comet since it was accelerating, and up to 10 times as long as it was wide. These items could create interstellar impacts as well.

2. It gives us more information about our solar system, galaxy, and universe.

When we take on the effort to start exploring space, then we can discover new truths about our planet and culture simultaneously. The information we obtain from these studies can then be applied to our STEM resources here at home. NASA technologies that were originally developed for space programs include infrared ear thermometers, LED lighting, ventricular-assist devices, anti-icing systems, and even temper foam. Because it requires us to innovate to reach to the stars, our efforts to solve critical problems create opportunities to make life better here on our planet at the same time.

3. Exploring space is one of the few human endeavors that crosses borders.

There are currently 72 countries who claim to have a space program, but there are only three which have an operating government space agency: China, Russia, and the United States. Despite the political conflicts that occur between these nations, their capability of producing human spaceflight provides the gold standard for future exploration efforts. Only 14 of the 72 nations who operate in this space even have a basic launch capacity and six (adding Europe, India, and Japan) have the capability to launch or recover multiple satellites. Because of the expenses and resources necessary to achieve space flight, the remaining nations work together with those who have the capability of a full launch to manage this aspect of human existence. This endeavor is one of the few ways that humans from all nations cooperate without conflict.

4. We can see humanity in a different way with space exploration.

Carl Sagan suggested that Voyager 1 take a picture of Earth while it was 4 billion miles away at more than 30 degrees above the ecliptic plane. In that image, our planet appears as a 0.12 pixel crescent. All of our conflicts, political battles, successes, failures, love, loss, and life occur on this one-tenth of a pixel. In the scope of a universal lens, we are but one small point of light amount countless others.

"Look again at that dot," wrote Sagan. "That's here. That's home. That's us. On it everyone you love, everyone you know, everyone you ever heard of, every human being who ever was, lived out their lives. The aggregate of our joy and suffering, thousands of confident religions, ideologies, and economic doctrines, every hunter and forager, every hero and coward, every creator and destroyer, every king and peasant... every saint and sinner in the history of our species lived there – on a mote of dust suspended in a sunbeam."

5. Space exploration provides us access to new raw materials or undiscovered natural resources.

When we began to launch satellites into space, it allowed us to find new raw material deposits on our planet that we could access to make life easier here. If we apply this technology as an extension to the rest of our solar system, then it gives us the same benefit to find minerals, precious metals, and even new materials that we can use. Although the expense of exploring space is admittedly high, this advantage gives us a way to offset those costs somewhat. There is even the potential that it could become profitable one day if we can provide these efforts with enough capital.

6. Investments into space exploration create real economic benefits at home.

The governments which provide the majority of our space exploration infrastructure employ over 20,000 people per agency who make direct positive economic impacts on their community. There are private companies who look at the potential benefits of this industry and contribute to this advantage as well, such as SpaceX and their thousands of staff. People from all walks of life contribute to space exploration every day, ranging from astronomers to actual rocket scientists. Even though many of these programs receive taxpayer funding, the wages, manufacturing, and indirect investments contribute over 70% more in overall value at the local level compared to each dollar spent in the United States. These opportunities allows us to explore many different fields of study in addition to what is waiting in the universe as well.

7. Anyone can become a space explorer to achieve their dream.

Space exploration doesn't need to involve starships, space stations, or intergalactic travel. If you own a telescope and can look up at the sky, then you can embrace this element of human existence. Our scientists have taken this advantage to the next level with the Hubble Space Telescope, which has made over 1 million observations in almost 30 years of service. We have made some incredible discoveries with this technology already.

•We have a better idea about the age of the universe (around 13.7 billion years).

•Images of the deep universe show that there are thousands of galaxies out there.

•It helped us to discover four of the five moons that orbit Pluto.

•We have a better understanding of planetary seasons in our universe.

•It works to peer into the atmospheres of alien planets so that we know what is waiting for us in our future exploration efforts.

8. Space exploration encourages us to share instead of being selfish.

Being human-first from a space exploration standpoint isn't about dominating other cultures that we might find waiting for us in the universe. It is a way for us to find common ground outside of our physical appearance, cultural differences, or religious preferences. For far too long, we have allowed ourselves to be consumed by our petty problems instead of looking at the big picture. If someone is hungry, then we should feed them. If they are cold, then we should clothe them. If they need a job, then we should help to train them. Space exploration unites us in ways that other global efforts do not because we see ourselves as humans first. This advantage won't solve our problems, but it can shift our attitude toward something that is healthier than our current state.

9. We know more about our planet thanks to our efforts to explore space.

Because space exploration gives us a different perspective, it allows us to look at our planet in a different way. The view from outside of our atmosphere allows us to see the big picture instead of trying to extrapolate information from micro-scale research. This advantage allowed us to discover the problem of ozone depletion in the upper atmosphere, begin the conversations on global warming, and examine the current and future impact of weather pattern changes that may happen because of a changing climate. Space exploration helps us to look inward as well as outward, helping us all to find the changes that are necessary to keep our planet healthy for our children, grandchildren, and beyond. But, space exploration also have these disadvantages, they may include as below:

1. Our current technology makes it dangerous to get into space in the first place.

Several agencies are developing "space tourism" packages that can take people in a comfortable aircraft to the very outer layers of our atmosphere, but that is not an exploration effort. We currently strap astronauts into a vehicle that gets attached to a very large rocket so that there is enough speed available to break the grasp of gravity.

Starting with Theodore Freeman, who was killed in the crash of a T-38 in October 1964, there have been over 20 individuals who lost their lives in the line of duty while advancing U.S. space program interests. There have been two individuals (Gus Grissom and Peter Siebold) who were able to survive a problem that resulted in the loss of a space vehicle.

2. There are cost considerations to look at with space exploration.

The cost of exploring space is one of the biggest criticisms of the efforts to launch a program that takes us beyond our planet. When the space shuttle program was active in the United States, the total cost of the launch was about $500 million. That figure does not include the expenses of postponement that often occurred because the conditions were not right to send a rocket into space.

Manned missions in our solar system could cost 10 times that amount, and that might get us to Mars or one of Jupiter's moons. Technology advancements in recent years could make this issue cheaper for the next generation, but we should ask ourselves if spending billions on space exploration is the right thing to do if we have people dying of hunger on our planet.

3. Astronauts receive exposure to natural dangers while in space.

If the launching process doesn't kill you during a manned space exploration effort, then the natural dangers that are present outside of our planet's atmosphere could become problematic in a variety of ways. The radiation that comes from the sun is a constant danger to astronauts when they are in space, and the weightless environment can change their physical conditioning. Experiments with identical twins, with one staying on our planet and the other spending a lengthy assignment in space, show that there are changes at the cellular and genetic level that occur with space travel as well.

4. Current space exploration efforts could be a one-way trip.

When we sent astronauts to the moon, our technology provided them with a chance to land on the surface and return to their spacecraft. It is possible that we could perform a similar action for asteroids, moons around other planets, and other celestial bodies that do not have an atmosphere. If we are going to start exploring Mars, then that journey could be a one-way trip for the astronauts. Even if this journey does not become a one-way trip, the amount of time necessary to reach a destination beyond the moon makes it virtually impossible to mount a rescue mission if something goes wrong. Our current vision of space exploration requires perfection to create a successful result.

5. There may not be a reason to start exploring at this time.

Human cultures have always had a fascination with exploring space because it satisfies our need to learn more about the universe. Taking long-distance pictures with the Hubble telescope is not the same as visiting the location in-person. What we must ask ourselves right now is if there is a valid reason to begin this effort, and the truth is that there are few pragmatic applications to consider. We could start mining asteroids for their raw materials and mineral content in the future. Planetary colonization could be necessary in future generations. Since we are still dealing with issues like crime and poverty here at home, addressing our immediate concerns might be better than looking at future needs which might never be necessary.

6. Unmanned probes are even a waste of resources.

One of the ways that we attempt to limit expenses with our space travel needs is to send unmanned probes into the dark vastness that lies beyond. There have been some successes with these efforts, most notably the Voyager 1 and Voyager 2 missions that allow us to peer outside of our solar system. This option allows us to almost eliminate the risk to human life entirely as well. There are also disadvantages to consider with this approach, starting with the fact that there is little adaptability to changing circumstances. The Mars Climate Orbiter is an excellent example of this problem. When it received incorrect coordinates for landing, it burned up while entering the atmosphere before sending any data at a cost of more than $120 million.

7. Our current information is well out-of-date.

On February 22, 2017, NASA announced that it had found seven planets the size of Earth in a single solar system. Three of the planets were in the so-called Goldilocks Zone, which means they are at a distance from their star that is not too hot and not too cold. It is called the Trappist-1 group, and this set of planets lies in the Aquarius system. That's about 235 trillion miles away, which is at least a measurable distance.

The problem is that this planetary system is 40 light-years away from us. That means the information that we can observe right now took forty years to get to our scientists. Think about all of the changes that have happened in your life in just the past 5 years, and then apply that concept to a planetary scale. When we start exploring space, we must take into account that this delay is present so that we don't fly into an unexpectedly dangerous situation.

8. It may lead us into future conflict with beings who have superior technology.

Space exploration makes us think in noble terms about what lies in wait for us in the universe. When we sent the Voyager spacecraft into our solar system and beyond, there were two records placed on the devices to communicate with whoever might find them to let that intelligent life know that we exist. Most theorists who seriously consider the pros and cons of meeting alien life say that there are only two possible outcomes that can occur with first contact. That alien species will either be so advanced that their technological presence as led to a peaceful society where an exchange of information may one day be possible, or it will be aggressive and want to access our planetary resources.

9. Space exploration creates a lot of trash or rubbish around our planet.

There are over half-a-million items of trash from over 50 years of space travel and satellite placement which orbit our planet right now. Unless these items fall into the atmosphere and burn up, they will stay in place forever. The ring of debris that we have created makes space exploration more dangerous because an impact with a ship's hull could have deadly results. We will need to clean up this mess in the future to provide better safety to our future explorers, and we have no idea what the expense might be.

Verdict ( comparison) on the Advantages and Disadvantages of Space Exploration

Space exploration is beneficial even if we only look at it through the lens of hope. It is an idea that unites us as one race instead of over 190 different countries. We can proceed into the universe as one people, taking the first steps toward new experiences just like we did when we placed astronauts on the moon for the first time. Explorers always face danger, and space is no exception to that rule. The vacuum of the universe was not meant for humans, which means we must constantly adapt and protect ourselves when we are outside of our atmosphere. Then there is the risk of an encounter with alien life to consider too.

The advantages and disadvantages of space exploration must come from a common sense perspective. Other races could harm us, but there is also the possibility that we could be dangerous to other life as well. We should continue with these efforts, but with the understanding that this work is not a race. It is a cooperative effort that will eventually define our humanity.

Similarity, space exploration's benefit and risk may include as these: The benefits of space exploration is it helps man think outside the box as far as the dwindling resources are concerned. The risk is that it can lead to death. The only drawbacks are cost and safety. If you can afford the cost and are willing to take the risk, there are unlimited benefits. To further our knowledge on the ever expanding universes. However, there are so many problems that are associated with space exploration. Some of the problems include the high costs, the risk level is also very high and there are chances of getting negative results. But, space exploration also have these intangible benefits , such as the benefits are that it has more space and more fuel than the Apolo and it gives astronauts a chance to bring whole satilities. Space stations can help in the exploration of space because in space stations they do experiments on things they find in space.


How does space exploration impact us?
Beyond furthering the scientific understanding of how the universe formed, the mechanics involved in galatic, solar, and planetary formations, as well as mapping the universe for potential physical exploration at a later date, the space exploration programs impart a bevy of technologies which are applied to everyday use as well as research benefits that come from zero gravity research (such as medicines or materials development. The commercial impact seen from the space program can be possible brought to our next

generation in the future. What are the reasons for space exploration? In conclusion, I feel that space exploration may bring these intangible benefits. they may include: Space exploration is an important part of our life today. The main reasons for exploring space are: The urge to know what is out there as well as by space exploration, we get to know if there is any harm from the heavens coming our way. Thus, space exploration will bring future intangible and tangible benefits more than present risk. Space scientists ought concentrate more nervous, time , human and technological resources to research how to achieve this space exploration mission more than space travel. Due to space travel present and future risk is more than future benefit as below reasons.

What are the benefits and risks of space travelling? I shall indicate as below:

What is space travel benefit ? Nowadays, human begins feel space travel is one kind of exciting entertainment activity, instead of earth travel. But, due to space travel cost is high, so this kind of travel activity is focus on rich people because they have more extra money to spend this kind of travel entertainment. It is its weakness. Space is fascinating. Humans have been sending objects into space for decades, trying to learn about Earth and what's beyond. But while space travel can be beneficial, there are also risks that come along with exploring the rest of the universe. There have been many more trips to space and the moon, as well as orbits around Earth. Our fascination with the universe beyond our own planet is as limitless as the universe itself. Technology and science have even allowed us to land on and explore Mars - a feat barely imaginable when space travel first began decades ago.

However, space travel also have these kinds of different risks when space travelers are flying rockets to space. The different risks may include as below:

(1) Health risk

The Health Risks of Space Travel

,research into the health risks of space travel may someday make long-duration spaceflights safer for astronauts. But despite such achievements, space travel still involves a myriad of health risks for people. From DNA damage caused by radiation exposure to the bone loss, muscle loss, and blood pressure changes that occur when living in microgravity, to name a few.

(2) Radiation risk

Also, space travel can bring radiation risks. The latest review examines eight NASA evidence reports, with half of the topics focused on the health risks of radiation exposure in space. "The radiation problem is the toughest one to solve and the most concerning," Valerie Neal, Ph.D., a historian at the National Air and Space Museum, told Health line. Neal spent 10 years working at NASA, but she was not involved in the current research. On Earth, Neal explained, we are shielded by the planet's magnetic field and the protective gases in the atmosphere.

However, there's no effective way to shield astronauts from some types of radiation present in space, especially on a long journey such as a trip to Mars.

In particular, there is no technology to protect against galactic cosmic rays, a type of ionizing radiation likely produced by supernovae, or exploding stars. That type of radiation can pass right through the hull of a spacecraft and the skin of people on board.

Astronauts also face radiation risks from solar particle events, which are difficult to predict.

In its current review, the National Academies' committee looked at NASA's evidence reports on radiation exposure and increased risk of cardiovascular disease, cancer, central nervous system disorders, and acute radiation syndrome. For the conditions covered in each report, the committee noted that NASA has well-documented evidence of the risks, although some studies rely heavily on animal models. One area of growing interest is the link between radiation and cardiovascular disease. The committee found that there's now enough evidence, "to support the conclusion that the risk of degenerative diseases from long-term exposure to space radiation may be of much greater concern than previously believed."

(3) Cancer risk

Space travel also brings cancer risk.

Another major area of concern is cancer.

Radiation exposure can cause genetic damage that may increase an astronaut's risk of developing cancer years after their mission.

Currently, NASA sets the radiation limit for astronauts at a 3 percent cancer fatality probability. For a mission on the ISS, where proximity to Earth provides some protection from radiation, women can stay about 18 months and men can stay about 24 months before exceeding the limit. But on a mission to Mars, astronauts would be way over the limit, according to Francis Cucinotta, Ph.D., a professor of health physics at University of

Nevada, Las Vegas, who authored the research on exposure limits.
Cucinotta worked for NASA for more than a decade, and developed a database that tracks astronauts' exposure to radiation and cancer risk estimates. He told Health line it would be a question of ethics whether to raise the risk limit to allow astronauts to travel to Mars.

(4) Mental illness risk

But the hazards of space aren't the only risks astronauts face on a long voyage.
They also have to put up with each other, while maintaining their own sanity in a small, cramped space. The National Academies also examined NASA's evidence reports on mental health issues related to space travel and "behavioral health decrements" when team members aren't working well together.
Another report focused on the health risks associated with sleep loss, circadian rhythm issues, and work overload. Lastly, the committee reviewed evidence on risks related to "vestibular/sensorimotor alterations," which include issues like space motion sickness. Overall, the committee noted that all of NASA's reports were quite thorough, but recommended that NASA pay more attention to the interactions between different types of risks. For example, lack of sleep and being overworked could have a big impact on how well a team of astronauts works together. Teamwork issues are especially important to consider on long-duration missions, according to Neal.

"On a one- to two-week mission you are so busy, you don't have time for interpersonal issues to form," Neal told Health line. But on longer missions, more psychological factors come into play. She noted that being able to call family and friends back home and talk in real time has made a world of difference for astronauts' mental health and well-being.
But those immediate connections wouldn't be possible on a long mission to Mars — which could be a real source of stress for astronauts.

In conclusion, although, space travel is one kind of exciting and new travel entertainment activity, however, it can only let some rich people can enjoy the short time space travel journey. So, poor people won't enjoy this kind of travel entertainment. But, it also bring different risks when space travellers are catching the rocket to fly to the space anywhere to travel. Moreover, any space travellers have life danger when they are catching the rocket to fly to space anywhere to travel, even the cost is expensive, e.g. space travel facility, space travel destination entertainment arrangement.

They need spend too much money to build on the planet when the space travellers arrive the planet to travel. If the space travelling investor can not gain any reward to compensate their expenditure, then they will encounter much loss. Is it still worth to invest more than space exploration? Otherwise, if any space exploration is successful, then it may bring another earth existence in possible and human may attempt to live another planet in possible. So, it seems that space exploration can bring long term benefit more than space travel because space travel is one kind short time individual entertainment enjoyable benefit. Otherwise, space exploration is one kind long time human overall living benefit. It explains that why exploring space is more important than exploring space travel.

Mars exploration failure factors

What are Mars exploration possible failure factors? I shall indicate Mars exploration mission possible failure reasons as below:

On space exploration improvement aspect: US plans for the human exploration of Mars are best seen as a serious human spaceflight effort. It is possible that improvements in technologies will make flights to Mars feasible and survivable, but these technologies are still in development. Robotic exploration provides the scientific benefits to be gained from exploring Mars at lower cost and much lower risk. When these is a manned flights to Mars, serious political interest is lacking. A manned mission to Mars is not likely to occur for at least 10 years, if not longer.

The problem may include: How to provide fast speed space station transportation service between earth and Mars, less dangerous risk or high safety, providing more innovative space manned flight activities lead to space tourism or some other commercial activity involving human spaceflight. Acquiring earth observation satellites for security purposes, providing imagery, electronic intelligence and communications services, spacecraft, robotic and more advanced space shuttles, ability to maneuver in orbit, remain in space for long periods. So, space technology must need to be improved if space scientists hope to explore Mars to achieve to let human to live in possible in future one day.

On space science continue researching and development aspect: Why do space scientists need to continue space science research, if they hope to explore Mars more easily? Because we live in a society which depends on science and technology, those are very essentials seem undervalued perhaps because they are not understood. There are great concern in some quarter about the inadequacies and shortcomings in science funding, science education and the way space science in communicated to the public. For these questions example: Why do we need to choose Mars to live? How do we need explore Mars to live in success? What benefits and risks do we encounter in this Mars exploration process? So, space scientists have responsibilities to let pubic to know because they need people vote to support their Mars exploration mission. If people do not understand engine science , space science, medical science or whatever, then they are not equipped to get knowledgeably on science issues.

In space science, there are two main but not necessarily separate for spending, sometimes referred to collectively as research and development. Research is the acquisition of new knowledge. Development is the application of existing knowledge to new or improved user, such as exploration continue research of any new space exploration knowledge to Mars as well as they also need to learn how to apply existing Mars exploration knowledge to new or improved uses. However, there is no way of knowing where or when any kinds of new Mars exploration knowledge will find a practical application. But they need still continue to research and develop any possible new kinds of Mars exploration new technology.

However, researching and development is impossible without approval and funding. It is safe to say. Then, that some of the most vital work done, such as Mars exploration by space scientists is in preparing their funding applications. Also, space science is a around field, with a vary limited number of resources for cutting edge research. An idea for research and there is a fair chance that someone has already thought or it is already working on other similar earth seven planets , or other undiscovered researching planets which choice has higher successful chance to implement human living another earth mission. So, choice of which one space exploration mission is the best, it needs space scientists compare their benefits and risks in order to make final space exploration decisions.

On space exploration expenditure spending aspect: NASA needs to make budget for everything from launching missions to conducting educational programs, such as human space flight, which includes the shuttle and space station, gets around bit billion of that. Space missions are cheaper today than in earlier times, because the technology is in general cheaper and methods have been improved.

Billion dollar figures naturally keep a lot of people in work, and have an economic influence, but are there tangible returns that the ordinary citizen can consider over the entire range of space based activity, such as whether exploration of Mars mission is the most reasonable choice among other planet exploration choices? How will serious economic effect be influenced by this wrong failure space mission decision ?

One of the first and most obvious results of the space age was the rapid progress in satellite and communications technology, evident today is so many aspects of life that our interface with them is virtually seamless. What is the value of satellites? From weather reports, sports broad casts, and communication networks to geographic information systems, geophysical research and the global positioning system, we can earn the benefits of the space age every day of our lives. If nothing else had some of the space race, we would still have different reasons. In fact, that satellite technology has become a commercial enterprise means that it can pay its own way.

What do we get for our investment in space? The space environment offers conditions of microgravity, vacuum, and temperature extremes, which hold promise for experiments and possess not possible on earth. The vacuum of space , for example is better than the best vacuum attainable on earth. So , space scientists need to find methods how to flight this natural and dangerous space environment, it includes radiation, simulate, progress in developing more versatile , and efficient materials and engineering methods. However, these developments can bring indirect benefits to our space exploration development, such as computers, medical equipment and electronics science in general have all benefited from the space exploration development age.

However, space scientists need to make an analysis of the likely risks and benefits of any one space exploration research. There must be interested to know, for instance, how his/her idea would almost certainly to choose the planet living exploration, any planet living explorations must be at same stage , the come a point where the benefits outweigh the risks and the financial budget can be justified.

Deciding whether a risk is acceptable is necessarily subjective, such as the Mars exploration mission. Rocket testing is done in isolated areas, and launch paths or usually over wide stretches of ocean or sparsely populated land, when the rocket arrives the Mars land. It must need ensure safe and none crash or fire occurrence accident when the rocket arrives on the Mars land. Costly through a failure is the risks in unmanned missions are relatively strategic involving fire or pollution from rocket fuel , and falling space junk. Onboard radioactive substances can certainly give valid cause for concern, but once a craft has left earth orbit, the space men are out of danger, when their rocket arrives on the Mar's land.

By comparison with radio active,if you feel rocket fuel and space plane quickly, the risks do seem minimal probably, they are. We should put those possibilities into perspective, through, e.g. tens of thousands od people live in close proximity to airports, and face the prospect of having a burning airbus coming down coming down on top of them. It is something we live with, such as our solution concerns how to the Mars, when it only has one limit number of space station to let the rocket to land on Mars, and it can not cause any fire occurrence to bring life absolutely dangerous to our life, if we were living on the Mar's land one day. For instance, that microscopic organisms can survive and mutate in the microgravity and higher radiation levels of space stations.

What would happen if Mars people came back to Earth as passengers on an astronaut's clothing? Moreover, we must rightly consider the possibility of dangerous Martian microbes arriving on Earth in samples returned by robot explorer. Will quarantine conditions devised around known standard be sufficient? Suppose some of our own bacteria travel to Mars on our spacecraft survive on the surface, but mutate in the intense UV radiation. What kinds of diseases could they cause when human explorers arrive ?

In conclusion, mutant Earth bacteria will have to be dealt with of and when they are encountered. The possibility of native microbes from Mars arriving, though is already taken seriously enough by some people that an organization dedicated to seeing that samples are not returned is already in existence. Another problem is how adaptable living on Mars problem, how can human adapt to live in Mars in the silence of space environment , but it would be too much for modern city, light weight feeling when human does not need to walk on Mars' land. All of these issues will be human need to face problems, if space scientists can confirm Mars can be one adaptable planet to let us to live to compare other planets in the future possible one day.

● Space exploration possible
economic benefits

What are economic benefits of space exploration? Space exploration may bring these economic benefits as below: The critical drive of technological changes linked to the space industry. Firms may make technological leap that took billions in public funds to finance to carry on continue space exploration research continue in long term into the different kinds of space markets development, e.g. space resource exploration, space living environment exploration, space energy exploration , space tourism expenditure exploration etc.

For new entrants to all one space market, they may be assisted to invest to build their own rocket factories or space stations , how to design and rebuild reusable rockets easily when they anticipate to any kinds of space exploration activities. It can increase cooperation to develop future space exploration missions successful chance as well as expertise is increasingly consolidated within single firms, instead of across a multiplicity of vendors and contractors. Because any one space exploration activity, if there are many different countries' space exploration companies anticipate , it will bring more success in the process of designing, testing and improving products in all those space exploration companies in new and innovative ways.

Then, any one space exploration mission success, it also brings another or other new technological business chance. It helps to create monopolies or at least oligopoly and this provide sufficient incentive to innovate or drive down costs to US space industry sells its any space exploration products into international market as well as creating more space exploration manufacturing workers, space products salespeople, space science teacher etc. positions job opportunity to reduce unemployment ratio and encouraging more students choose space science subject to learn. It can change to the space exploration industry with long-term commercial, scientific and even military security, technical innovation economic benefits to global entrepreneurs, even when any one space exploration technological development reaches mature stage, then it will bring long term profits, as reducing cost and less risky businesses in possible.

In conclusion, it seems that space exploration industry may bring long term economic benefits more than long term economic loss. It depends on this factor whether how many space exploration technological firms can be encouraged to cooperate together. When any one space exploration activity/mission has many space exploration firms anticipation, then the space exploration activity/mission will have high successful chance. Otherwise, there are less number space exploration firms cooperate to carry on researching the space exploration activity/ mission, then it will have high failure chance. Some firms anticipative number will be one important influential factor to any one of space exploration activity/mission.

● THE PROBLEM OF SPACE LABS AND SPACE STATIONS EXPENDITURE

By these estimates and assumptions, research labs and space stations would need at least 25 modules to be profitable at any point in their operational lifetime. The ISS has less than this but was not designed to be profitable and is not entirely used for research. As launch costs decrease over time, smaller space stations will be economically feasible and more likely to attract investors. Until this ,

however, large space stations will likely be the only ones considered and such a large capital investment most likely rules out private ventures. Lab revenues, which were fixed for this analysis, are actually more likely to vary than launch cost and could greatly distort these trends.

● THE PROBLEM OF ENOUGH NATURAL RESOURCE SUPPLY ON THE SUSTAINABILITY OF SPACE COLONY

Although the focus now is on how a space colony can be made feasible, the underlying challenge is to make such a colony sustainable. Since the purpose of a colony is to be a long term habitat for humans, then the primary task is to work up to the point when this is possible. A large part of making a colony sustainable is having enough energy and resources to maintain human life and support the activities that the colony was created for.

The main purpose of a colony highly affects these requirements.

A research colony would most likely consist of a medium number of living inhabitants and a significant amount of laboratory and observation equipment. For this settlement, a moderate amount of food would be needed along with a substantial energy source. A mining colony, on the other hand, would consist of heavy machinery, robots and far fewer humans to act as supervisors. Despite needing less food to

sustain this type of colony, a much greater amount of energy would be needed. Finally, if we consider a space ecosystem that's main purpose was to facilitate human inhabitants, the food and nutritional requirements would be a major

concern while energy levels could be low to moderate compared with the other colony applications.

Using the same three colony examples, it is necessary to also compare the required interactions with earth. For this comparison it must be

assumed that colonies cannot provide their own food and that these resources
must be sent from earth. Also, communication and any sharing of ideas or information are also considered interactions with earth. If these were not true and a colony could provide for itself then it would most likely already be feasible and sustainable.


Research colonies would need frequent interactions with earth to share new ideas and test out concepts on earth. Since only a medium amount of food is essential to sustaining this colony, the frequency of communication visits would be more than sufficient to transport all needed food and resources. For the mining settlement, there would only need to be somewhat frequent trips from space to earth and vice versa to send the mined resources
to earth and the required food to space. Communication for anything other than emergencies would be minimal because
the people in control of the operation would most likely be in space supervising the operations.

A purely human colony would call for the most interaction with earth because of the high amount of food and resources required on a daily basis. This type of colony is the hardest to make sustainable. This is due to the fact that there are more humans who need to be kept alive and there is no source of profit to guarantee the feasibility of sustained efforts. From a humanitarian standpoint
ultimate to sustain prolonged human life outside of the earth's ecosystem. It is also the most advanced and expensive colony and it's the farthest off from becoming possible in the future.

Because of this, the very first colony is almost certainly going to be similar to a mining
operation on earth. This would be the most profitable out of the three types, and also the most simple technologically. Such a establishment in space could be used to test out bioengineering advances so that
eventually humans will have the capability to stay in space for longer and longer periods of time, working up to the when a non-profitable human settlement is possible long term.

Propulsion is by far the most significant contributor to making a colony initially feasible,
but it contributes little to making that same colony sustainable. Bioengineering becomes the more important aspect of technological

advancement because the protection of human life is the most challenging problem regarding long term stays in space. Commercialization also plays an important role because the sustained funding for these expensive colonies cannot realistically come from government budgets or private investments. If a colony does not have a commercial motive, then it is that much harder to not only sustain but to start in the first place. This is the main reason why a colony for only humans is so difficult to establish.

● THE PROBLEM OF WHETHER HUMAN CAN ADAPT OR ADOPT TO LIVE IN NATURAL SPACE PLANET ENVIRONMENT IN LONG TERM

In order to fully understand the detrimental effects that space has on humans,

testing would need to focus on the aspects of the earth's environment that differ most with those in space. First, humans are very susceptible to radiation so they would either need to be highly protected, or treated that radiation does not have as much of a negative effect on the body. Humans would also have to withstand great temperature variations in space if a suitable environment could not be designed.

Our chemical makeup would have to change severely if unprotected humans would be able to withstand the harsh temperatures of our solar system. Certain pressures would also have to be maintained in order for our bodies to function normally as they do on earth. The levels of gravity take a toll on human bones and muscles as well, and would have to be increased in space for us to exist for long periods
of time.

Finally, light is a very important but often overlooked factor that contributes to the function of the brain. In order to maintain sanity and normal biological processes, humans in space would need to get the right amount of sunlight. Many of these variables could be tested in the extreme environments on earth to see how
different levels affect the human body, but eventually the research would have to be continued in space to see how versatile our body truly is.

● THE PROBLEM OF SPACE TECHNOLOGICAL IMPROVEMENT

With improved technology in the future, less fuel can be used to achieve the same velocity so it will be possible to use single stage propulsion for comparable missions. Selection of the optimal chemical fuel has provided many challenges in the past because of the vast
tradeoffs between available possibilities. Hydrogen is preferred because it

is very prevalent on earth and can be easily burned with oxygen. It is also has a great combustion efficiency, cooling abilities, and low condensed mass compared to other fuels. Although it has the highest thrust to mass ratio of any rocket fuel, it requires very large and heavy fuel tanks which make the structural design of the vehicle much more difficult. This also is a huge setback to decreasing the structure to overall mass ration that is required to make SSTO possible. Therefore future single stage rockets using chemical propellants will not use hydrogen unless a better way to store it is discovered. The space technological challenges may include as below:

For a spacecraft with this weight delivering human to space technological transportation tool example, difference in theoretical maximum payloads is 5000 kilograms. This may not seem like a big difference, but it is remarkable. This extra space could be worth as much as $100 million, which is also the same amount of revenue that was assumed to be needed to attract investors. This would be possible if the payload was used to transport goods made in space to be sold and used on earth. All of the estimates and assumptions used to obtain these values are the same as in the Launch Cost Economics analysis.

Propulsion and transportation have always been one of humanity's greatest challenges and triumphs. Many of the great innovations that have allowed humans to evolve and flourish have come in these fields. The development of SSTO technology opens endless possibilities for the human race and would greatly expand the perceivable universe to humans. A breakthrough of that magnitude would certainly be one
of the most significant in modern history. The ability to access space frequently with the purpose of improving humanity is the pinnacle of human achievement. For this reason, advances in propulsion are fundamental to prolonged human presence in space.

For solar power technological energy resource example, the initial steps of commercializing space would either
involve energy or manufactured goods. The profitability and continuous demand for these would ensure a successful space business if the product could be transported to earth. SSTO propulsion would allow for the cheap and regular transportation of the final product and would greatly reduce the costs associated
with doing business in space. The commercialization of space is a critical element in the possibility of a space colony, because the only way human activity in space will increase enough is if there is a profit to be made.

Solar power arrays in space are a promising business opportunity and could be one of the first business venues involving energy. They are unique because, similar to satellites, they do not require a colony in space to be possible. Although the mining of Helium-3 would represent an extremely profitable and beneficial

source of energy, the labor source and supervision necessary would guarantee that a colony would need to be created to sustain such a long term operation. When studying commercialization as a step in the process

towards colonization, opportunities like this should not yet be considered.

● THE FINAL PROBLEM OF SAFE ENVIRONMENT LIVING CHALLANGE

WHAT IS SPACE ENVIRONMENT PROTECTION AND SAFETY ?

One of the greatest possibilities for humans in space is also one of their greatest obstacles.

It is the effect that being in space has on the human body and how humans can adapt to different environments. There are several naturally occurring reactions that take place within the human body when it is kept in space

for extended periods of time. Although it is unknown if these are the body's adaptations to space or if space is causing the body to transform, this shows that some configurations of life work better in space. This offers great

promise for bioengineering because after these transformations have been studied, scientists could engineer the human body to take on these desirable conditions. The body will need to react to different conditions quickly in order to

become better suited for life in space. This research will greatly expand the possible lifetime of humanity as a whole, whether it is by staying on earth or by venturing into space permanently. Although bioengineering may not significantly

speed up the race to colonize space, it will most assuredly make that colony possible and be a major factor in its success.

Within bioengineering and medical research in space there are a great deal of possible contributions to the improvement of

humanity. First, the limiting factor in space travel now is the amount of time that the human body can survive in space. This is not only because of the issue of life-sustaining resources, but also the harmful effects of the space environment on the body. Aside from dieting and physical training, astronauts only protect themselves from the harmful effects of space while they

are actually in space. They could go through a medical regimen before space travel that targeted the undesirable effects

and would act as an initial barrier to limit any effects that were able to get by the in-space protection. Also, humans could be treated after they returned home to reduce the amount of harmful effects. Another possible way to protect humans while in space is a biological warning system. If the undesired effects of space are known then it is assumed that there

also exists a way to measure them and determine how much the human body can safely withstand. For the example of radiation,

something similar to a Geiger counter could be used to warn space travelers when they are nearing danger so that it could be

avoided. After much data is gathered from such devices, safe routes through space could be mapped out so that travelers could

avoid paths and locations that are substantially more harmful to them.

A key aspect of sustaining human life in space is creating an environment that is sustainable in space for long durations.

The main reason why humans thrive on earth is because earth's environment is very versatile and recycles nutrients and resources

so that life can flourish. Photosynthesis and plate tectonics are the two most important contributors to this on earth and

similar processes would have to be adapted to a space colony to ensure that life in space could be possible for a long period of time. An effective way to conduct this type of research is to have a group of scientists that live in space to perform

experiments in simulated environments. This will tell us more about how biology reacts to a given set of living conditions.

Three types of environments that would be especially helpful for testing are ones that models deep outer space, one that is

very similar to our environment on earth, and possible conditions that could be created for a human colony in space. The final environment would change slightly as more information is discovered because it would be somewhere

in the middle of the other two. This set of conditions is what designers would strive to replicate when establishing a colony

in space. The artificial environment would start out very close to the conditions in a space ship and through refinements and iteration would eventually be similar to those on earth.

Before starting a colony, numerous variations would have to be tested so that an optimal set of conditions could be identified. This is a form of evolution, but would have to be sped up so the humans in space would not die out before achieving a successful balance between body and environment.

In conclusion, despite the fact that the vacation industry would still not be a profitable or enticing business opportunity, it is worth noting the effect that a lower launch cost would have on the theoretical market. Once commercialization and a possible colony have been fully implemented, the costs will be reduced and the demand will skyrocket. Although orbital hotels will not lead the charge for commercialization of space, they will become a large industry generations after there is widespread human activity in space. Hence, it explains that US government needs to solve above these main challenges if it can not achieve space travelling development aim in success, then it will feel more challenges to develop space cities to let human to live in success, because development space is one short term achievement aim, but developing space city mission is absolute one long term achievement aim.

# CHAPTER FOUR

# Computer tool useful leisure Consumer Behavior

Why China's computer manufacturing and product development industry will be global leader to compete US computer dominant market.

Nowadays, China's computer industry is the largetest hardware producer production and experts is dominated by Taiwanese firms. It is also the second largest personal computer ( pc) market and domestic pc companies are top three sellers in global computer manufacturing and product development market. Forx example, Lenovo buys BM pc business in 2004 year. It implies US, IBM pc manufacturing leader can not dominate global computer market in possible in the future.

Reed Electronic Research, Yearbook Of World Electronic Data ( 2003) indicated that the leading computer producing countries of hardware production in US $millions and share share of total gogal production: The world region US was the global rank number one. In 1995 year, US had US $76,284 value, market value 26.5%. Then in 2000 year, US had increased up to US $ 90, 430 value, market share 24%. Till to 2003 year, US had fallen down to US $ 69,102 value, market share 21.7%. However, US hardware production was still the global rank number one , although its hardware production value had been falling down. But, the following second rank country, Japan and the third rank country, Singapore and the fourth rank country, Taiwan and the fifth rank county China which hardware production value could not exceed US till to 2003 year. However, although China had the lowest hardware production value US $5,600 to compare to among of these countries in 1995 year, but China had increased the value to US $65,000 and market share to 20.5%. Otherwise, Japan, Singapore and Taiwan value and market share had surprisingly fallen down below than

China value in 2003 year. Thus, it seemed that China will be a potential country to compete US hardware production industry after 2003 year.

Reed Electronic Research, Year book Of World Electronic Data ( 2003) also showed that these computer companies of China had these % of market share : Beijing Founder had 9.9%, Tsinghua Tongtang had 7.8%, dell had 7.2 % , IBM had 5.1% , HP had 4.8% of market share. Thus, it also seemed that China some computer companies will have impotant large market share percentage in global pc sale market. In the future, global hardware production and pc sale industry. China and Taiwan both countries will be one pc manufacturing and design and sale partner. The reason is that China and Taiwan had been the number one rank of markers of notebook pcs, motherboards, scanners, keyboards, add-on card optical drives, monitors and some network equipment etc. pc ( personal computer) relative computer function products. It seems that these both countries had co-operated to research any computer relative products to sell to global computer market. They are also the original design manufacturers ( DDMS) develop and manufacture over half the world's notebook pcs as well as their customers include all major branded pc vendors ( OEMS).

Taiwan Minstry Of Economic Affairs ( 2003) indicated Taiwan's top notebook ODMS include: In 2003 year volume ( thousands) Quanta had $8,500 sale volume thousands , for example, Quanta major OEM partners include Gateway, Dell, HP, IBM, Apple , Sharp, Sony, Fujitsu-Siemens ( F/S). Compal had $6,000 sale volume ( thousands) , Compal major OEM partners include Dell, HP, F/S, Toshiba, Acer. Thus, it also implied Taiwan had many small size and non famous brand of computer companies which choose to co-operate to be partners with some global large size and famous brand of computer companies to raise competitive effort in global computer market, such as Dell, IBM, HP, Gatway, Apple etc.

Thus, the future trend of computer new product manufacturing development will shift from US to Taiwan and SE Asia, then to China. However, what kind of knowledge work factors will be needed to China and Taiwan . In general, notebook manufacturing stages will include: The first process is design stage, it includes concept design, such as analyze need, create concept and set brand image as well as product planning, such as business case, specifications, industrial design and sourcing strategy. The second process is development stage, it includes design review steps, such as design review, such as mock-ups, electrical test as well as prototype build, such as commercial samples, integrated system test as well as pilot production, such as production process design, pilot. Final process is production stage, it includes mass production, such as ramp-up, volume production, production testing and global distribution as well as sustaining support, such as speed bump, component replacement, technical support and warranty support. Thus, I believe that China and Taiwan must own thee knowledge work skillful of computer design and development professionals who can assist these two countries how to innovate their future computer development to change global traditional computer model to be renew and innovate computer model in the future.

Due to computer industry's stages of development and manufacturing are closely linked , need manufacturability , testing of sample products, concept design and product planning stay together in lead markets and branded vendors, design and development can be separated organizationally and geographically. Thus, China and Taiwan choose to co-operate to exchange their different skill, such as either China has own more concept design and product planning skill or more development skill or more production skill. Then, China will choose either one of the most beneficial comparative advantage among of them. To bring this one of the most beneficial co-operative advantage to attract Taiwan to choose either one of the beneficial comparative advantage of skill, such as either design or development or producton to already co-operate to compete the Western developed country US together.

Thus, US won't be the global computer industry development leader if both US country famous and large employee number computer companies, such as IBM and Apple which choose to outsource their pc design and development and production skill to China and Taiwan both countries to help them to develop global computer design and development and production skill to be upgraded. Thus, I feel these both countries will plan how to co-operate to compete US to win the global computer industry leader position in the future.

Factors influence consumers' laptop purchases.

In the future, instead of global computer manufacters need to consider the design, development and production processes, who also need to consider what factors can influence consumers' laptop purchases. Because any consumers have much different computer model and brand to choose to make final decision to buy any computers. If the computer manufacturer can predict what factors will be whose weakness(es) to influence global computer consumers to change whose mind or attitude to choose to buy other brands of computers, then it won't lose its many old computer customer numbers and reduces it market share in global computer market share.

Nowadays, in general computer has three kinds to provide to global consumers to choose to buy , such as laptop, notebook computers, desktops. it seems that laptop and notebook computers and desktops will have different factors to influence any consumers to choose to buy any brand of computer products. Thus, computer indsutry can divide three consumer groups, such as ( stayers, satisfied switchers and dissatisfied switchers) of a computer company with respect to the factors influencing consumers' laptops or notebook computers or desktops purchases. However, I feel the factors can include such as core technicl features, post purchase services, prices and payment conditions, peripheral specification, physical appearance, value added features and connectivity and mobility seven main factors that are influencing consumers' laptop or notebook computer or desktop purchases in global computer industry market.

Ganesh et al., (2000) indicates the customer base of a company consists of three groups of consumers: stayers, satisfied switchers and dissatisfied switchers. Therefore, the consumers in this study replied to the question about whether the current brand that who were using was their first laptop brand or whether who had switched from a previous laptop brand. As a following question, consumers who had switched were asked to state the reason of why who switched from a previous laptop brand brand to their current brand. The options include overall dissatisfaction from the previous laptop brand and reasons other than dissatisfaction. Thus, computer companies need to know what factors influence either whose prior computer customers why who don't choose repeat to buy its any computer products or whose new potential computer customers why who don't choose to buy its any computer products in the first time choice. Thus, future computer manufacturers need to consider intangible salespeople service attitude or performance, such as salespeople current purchase and post purchase service, e.g. technical repair, model function explanation how to use the computer, instead of tangible product performance, e.g. computer appearance design , function , mobility and internet and document download speed connectivity function. Because salespeople and technicians' service performance can be represented to the computer image. If they can provide excellent service to let computer buyers to feel satisfactory, then they can help their computer company employer to build good image. So, staff service performance will be one important factor to influence computer consumers to make the final decision to choose to buy the brand of computer products more easily. Even, one famous brand computer company, such as IBM, Apple, Gateway, these any one of famous brand computer company must not attract any new ( the first time) or repeat computer buyers to choose to buy their any kind of computer products , such as laptop, desktop or notebook more easily due to their famous brand. Althoug, these famous computer companies had built good image to let consumers have more confidence to buy any kind of their computer products. But, if these famous computer companies' salepeople or repair technicians can not provide excellent customer service or performance to satisfy their computer buyers' service need, e.g. explaining how to use the new computer, repair post purchase service etc. I believe these famous brands of computer consumers will not have more desire to prefer to chose to buy any one of these famous computer brand's products. Otherwise, if the other less famous computer companies' any kind of laptop, desktop or notebook sale price is higher than the famous brand of computer companies' products sale price, but their salepeople or technicians can provide more excellent service attitude or performance to satisfy their consumers' needs. It is possible that the new or first time computer buyers or repeat computer buyers will still choose to buy their computers. So, the famous or less famous computer brand is not one important factor to influence the computer buyer to decide either to buy the computer or not buy the computer. Otherwise, computer company's salepeople and repair technician whose service performance or attitude will be one important intangible factors to influence any first time ( new) or repeat computer consumers to choose to buy any famous or less famous brand of computer company's product, instead of the tangible computer design appearance and reliable function and convenient mobility and long term durability etc. factors influences.

Can culture factor influence the computer consumer choice?

Durmza and Zengin, (2011:53) indicted marketers closely interested in this issue to know the family which changed and renewed in course in time. It provides an advantage for a marketer to know the family structure and its consumption characteristics. Nowadays, consumer behavior is influenced not only by consumer personalities and motivation, but also by the relationships within families. Family is a social group and it can be considered a crucial place in th perception of marketing ( Durmaz, Yakup,

CELLK, Mucahit and ORUC, Reyhan, (2011).

The consumer buying behaviors examined through an empirical study. Then, it brings this question: Whether cultural factors will influnece the computer consumer choice. Choice and include computer brand choice, computer price choice, computer model choice, computer design choice, laptop or desktop or notebook product choice, new or second-hand old computer choice, the computer of manufacturing country choice, computer package choice etc. So, any consumer will consider to choose any one of these to decide to buy which kind of computer.

Every country computer consumers had different culture to influence their computer shopping choice. I feel culture can be explained how to influence to computer shopping such as: How do the country computer consumers buy and use their computer products habitually ? How do the country computer consumers react to th computer price changes, attractive advertising methods to satisfy whose needs and computer company store interiors? What underlying mechanisms operate to produce any one of the country computer consumers' responses? If computer marketers have answers to such these questions, who can make better managerial decisions how to adopt which computer target country ( countries) consumers' culture.

Consumer behavior deals with many other issues, for instance ( Priest, Carter and Statt, 2013: 19). How do we get information about products? How do we assess alternative products? How do different people choose or use different products? How do we decide on value for money ? How much risk do we take with what products? Who influences our buying decisions and our use of the product? How are brand loyalties formed and changed? For computer industry, it means that how computer consumers get information about computer products, how computer consumers assess alternative notebook, desktop, laptop computer products, how different age, country, culture, sex, student or working people or retired people computer consumers choose or use different kind of computer products, such as notebook, desktop, laptop computer products, how much risk computer consumers take with notebook, desktop, laptop computer products, the computer consumers' buying decisons and their use of the desktop or notebook or laptop computer products will be influenced by whom, e.g. family, friends, teacher, employer, computer salepeople, advertisement marketer etc. , computer company brands how are formed and changed by whom, e.g. computer consumers, computer company competitors, marketers, different countries' culture etc.

Durmaz and Jablonski, ( 2012:56) also explained culture is the essential character of a society that distinguishes it from other cultural groups. The underlying elements of every culture are the values, language, myths, customs, laws and the artifacts or products that are transmitted from one generation to the next ( Lamb, Hair and Deniel, 2011: 371). Culture is the most fundamental determinant of a person's wants and behavior. Whereas, lower creatives are governed by instinct, human behavior is largely learned. The child growing up in a society leans a basic set of values, perceptions, preferences and behaviors through a process of socialization involving the family and other social roles. So, I feel different country have different culture to influence as well as different country computer consumers who have different computer purchase and consume habitually. So, computer manufacturers ought focus on manufacturing the unique need and characteristics to satisfy any country's consumers' needs.

What is my idea about future global computer competition and factors influence computer consumer behavior ?

In conclusion, future computer industry development will trend that computer manufacturers need to consider every country's computer comsumer culture. Because every country computer consumers who will have different computer consumption habitually if who can predict what the country most computer consumers culture, then they can have more confidence to sell their computers to different country markets. Moreover, US computer manufacturers need to consider China and Taiwan computer manufacturing technology because it is possible that these both countries will be its main competitor among different computer manufacuring countries. Because thess both countries will cooperate to research new model of different computers to attract global computer consumers to choose to buy their new model of computer products in the future. Finally, computer manufacturers need to consider salepspeople and repair technicians service performance because computer consumers will consider intangible service performance , instead of tangible computer quality and price and style etc. factors . The main reason is that any computer have chance to be needed to repair and salespeople' skill will influence the computer consumer to make final decision to choose to buy the brand of computer. Thus, these factors will influence global computer development and trend in the future.

● Computer industry related service market development

What kinds of technologies innovation products will impact our future lives.

Europe in the 21 St Century is a technological society, how today technological trends could impact upon society in ways to be fully considered by clients' needs. What technological advancement products which can carry trend with it the promise of saving time, or assisting business or manufacturer industry clients to do more in the same amount of time.

In our clients buying choice view point, who ought hope any technological innovation products which can offer them that the opportunity to do things more efficiently. I shall suppose that technological innovation will be the main factor which can attract future many clients' purchase choice from the owned technological innovation product seller. For example, mobility, resource security , electronic government technological innovation products will be popular trend in future technological innovation product market.

● Autonomous automatic vehicle

Can autonomous vehicles be popular in the future driving market? Will your child soon be driving you to work? The autonomous vehicles ( artificial intelligent vehicles) will change the responsible driver concept. Why does autonomous vehicles will be future popular driving tools?

In fact, autonomous vehicles have these feature characteristics to differ to compare our common traditional driving tools. Their characteristics, such as real-time human control option, advantage of the large amount of high -quality mapping data of possesses to programing travel routes, exploring ways in which autonomous vehicle technology can be integrated with existing parking infrastructure to produce " driverless parking systems" accessible via existing personal electronic devices, e.g. smartphones is demonstrating the use of fully automated road transport systems in Europe and developing guidelines to design and implement such systems.

With some analysts predicting that by 2022 year , there will be around 1.8 billion automotive machine -to-machine connection its is clear that a large amount of data will be generated by vehicle in the future. Thus, this level of communication between automated vehicles should make to possible for such vehicles to navigate to destinations and interact with other vehicles and objects most effectively than a human brain. Moreover, they believe the chance of automatic vehicles' highway accidents occurrence will be less than traditional human driving vehicles.

Thus, the increased connectivity required to facilitate automation of vehicles would significantly improve the degree of monitoring of the performance of such vehicles. Individual owners would be able to better maintain and enhance their vehicles with improvements in fuel efficiency and lesser fuel spending and safety. This could also provide further benefits, such as terms of reducing traffic jams, reduced pedestrian exposure to pollution and lower risk of road-traffic and pedestrian incidents occurring, particularly in urban areas.

The rise of autonomous vehicles is also likely to combine with continuing electrification of vehicles as telecommunications software and hardware and further integrated into vehicles. Thus, the rental-orientated and purchase-orientated automatic vehicle business both models will have chance to be raised in future global driving market.

It causes the responsibility tends to lie with human drivers of vehicles will be decreased. A new set of IT skills in addition to a practical ability to drive and operate a more digital type of driving machine as well as it might impact upon existing vehicle users in terms of requiring re-training, particularly those less able to learn. Even, future public transport will have possible to be changed from non-human driving and change to automatic vehicle market will be individual and business both client markets in possible.

In conclusion, to success to sell non manual driving tools. The non manual driving sellers need to know how to solve these two artificial intelligent vehicles innovation questions: Could our future living habits change as a direct segment of changing transport behaviors? Will autonomous transport simply become and essential transportation tools for our homes and workplaces? Thus, if manufacturers want artificial intelligent vehicles sale number increases, which needs to influence future whose clients to accept this kind of non -human driving tools can be satisfy to change their traditional driving living habits for their new habit of non -manual driving method to substitute traditional manual driving tools.

● 3 D printer

Can 3 D printer be popular sale to manufacturing industry clients? What could be the effects to the physical environment and human health of such application 3D printer to copy to manufacture any productions? For example, medical equipment products, car keys, guns, furniture etc. different heavy or light weight manufacturing products.

The benefits to 3 D printer include: less production time, reducing purchase bulk or materials to produce any products, reducing to employ worker number to produce products, workers can learn to use 3D printer to copy to manufacture any products easily, to avoid air or water pollution to pollute working environment to influence worker health and safe production in factories, employers can pay less wages to employ less workers, workers can also raise more efficient during using 3 D printers to manufacture any products.

Thus, in the future 3 D printers can be popular to be used to copy to manufacture for these any products, e.g. jewelry or weapon industry products. In fact, 3 D printer is an additive manufacturing technology for making three- dimensional object, of almost one sharp using a digital model. Such as jewelry manufacturers apply it to copy to manufacture new kind of jewelry, hospitals can apply it to copy to manufacture any new medical equipment, weapon manufacturers can apply it to copy to manufacture any new gun weapons, aerospace or air plan manufacturers can apply it to manufacture new air plane engineering equipment or space exploration equipment or transportation tools. Thus, 3 D printer application will be popular to different aspects of manufacturing industry.

Future expected impacts and development for 3 D printer development. A macro economy level impact of 3 D printing will be considered to manufacturing industry business consumer-based economy and the societal behavioral acceptance in factories and offices manufacturing environment.

However, buying habits as individuals are able to print their own products, in comfort of their own home. Activity would be changed from traditional shopping methods to purchase 3 D printer to copy to manufacture own same products at home. Consumers can also choose how to design to print the product, rather than the manufacturing process itself is what consumers will be paying for and thus these is the potential for a design -lead choice behavior. Manufacturers don't need to buy many materials to manufacture products, they can use 3D printer , such as individual manufacturing machine parts, which could drastically improve their ability to design and manufacture more effective machine and components.

In conclusion, how to sell 3 d printer successfully. 3 D printer sellers need to know what advantages can give to 3 D individual consumption buyer and business buyer to let them to know to aim to let them to accept to change their buying behavior and manufacturing behavior for some products. There are some questions for consumers to attempt to answers:

What will the implications be the level of personal interactions between individuals in society of all of our products were to be manufacturing at home?

How would this change our typical buying habits and what would be the impact on our economy?

Would an increased use of 3D printing technology in the home or factory accelerate this process and what would be the implications for local high streets?

Would economies change being-focused will digital design skills having a greater benefits than traditional manufacturing methods?

If the ability to print everyday items at home becomes a reality , who is society would have the greatest access to such technology?

If a particular demographic section ( age, gender, race, income levels can be in factor to influence 3D printer consumer group, e.g. the 3 D printer buyer needs skills to manufacture any products, it seems only represented in a younger demographic. Could this mean that older members of society would not be able to benefit from 3 d printed projects?

In micro economy view point, although 3 D printer has benefits to individual and manufacturing consumers to reduce that their shopping or manufacturing expenditure, more design choice, raising worker individual skill and work performance. However, in macro economy view point, it also bring disadvantages to society. For example, if some members of society could not work move quickly, as a result than others, then what might be the impact upon their employability , e.g. causing unemployment of the 3D printer skillful learners who can not upgrade their working skill. Then, their employers will choose to dismiss these low skillful level 3 D printing learning skillful workers. Consequently, it will cause these member group of worker unemployment in the future society in possible. In conclusion, employers can not neglect how to train workers to learn how to apply 3 D printing skills to copy to manufacture any products.

● Massive open online course education

Will online education change traditional education? Basically, the students who choose to study from online channel, who must need have personal computers at home or school and often use internet from online platforms. In contrast to traditional methods of teaching with much small class size because every student can learn from online course at home. It means one teacher can choose to teach only one student from online channel. So, the teacher can stay at home or school as well as the student can stay at home , both of them can teach and learn from online teaching platform at the same time.

Whether the primary school, high school and university students who can accept to choose their learning habit to learn from this kind of online learning method more easily. In fact, online education will resultant impact on any teaching competitiveness. Due to , it is attempted to develop one kind of new technological education method to replace the traditional classroom by face -to-face teaching method between teacher and students contact.

However, it is not all course are suitable to adopt online teaching method and some courses re pointedly directed towards areas of interest that help education providers to also sell other online course products what other simply promote passive learning. For example, music, art, history, math, commerce courses which can be taught by teacher from online channel more easily. Because they do not need students to go to laboratory to do any experiments. Otherwise, engineering, food science, space science, medicine , doctor courses which need students go to laboratory to do experiments often. Thus, they are not suitable to be taught by teacher from online channel. Classroom teaching is more suitable to them.

Although, online teaching is low cost , due to that schools do not need many classrooms, even employ many teachers. So, they only buy computers and provide online education and less teachers are employed to teach whose students. So, it brings this question: Simply coursing cost barriers of success to education would not necessarily result in automatic take-up by young student consumers. May also need to think about best to education market, particularly to disadvantaged groups , such as older generations with lower computer and internet skills.

Who would be the winners and losers of an education market based upon such stronger principles of knowledge sharing and how can the institutions employing the use of such online or classroom or distance learning education methods be appropriately supported to maintain the high quality of further education? It seems to persuade students to choose online learning, the only method is that to let students feel online education can provide higher teaching quality level to compare traditional classroom learning method.

Other potential impacts of education market method relates more to education going online and a shift away from the more traditional forms of campus-based teaching in highest education . Would improving access to online education have the effect of increasing online students number. Due to who accept to choose online learning from traditional classroom learning habits . Thus, this is one learning habit change challenge for the traditional classroom learning students to adopt the online learning habit change.

In conclusion, for online education providers who need to consider how to change traditional classroom learning and teaching habit to adapt new online learning and teaching habit, as well as how to provide online teaching quality is higher level to compare to traditional teaching quality if who want their online education service businesses are successful.

● Future computer innovative and sustainable food source market

Future human considers health , so whose demand will high for quality of foods, farming of fish, typically freshwater with the cultivation of plants. It is simple future food source needs high health quality to provide to human to eat. If the food manufacture can have method to innovate any food quality to be more health to reduce poor health risk to influence human to eat. Thus, the food manufacturing process will be one important factor to attract consumers to choose to buy the food manufacturer's food supply. So, health food source market must attract many consumers to choose to buy to eat.

Computer technology can bring health foods supply method. Aquaponic system will be one health food manufacturing method. Aquaponic systems combine the farming of fish, typically freshwater, with the cultivation of plants. This takes place within a closed -loop aquaculture system, whereby fish are fed nutrients and their excrements one need as fertilizer directly into the water in which they are being loop. The water then feeds plants which use it for growth and filter the water , so it is suitable for re-use with the fish in the system. Such a system can be said to be closed-loop and hence a significant emphasis is placed upon the environmental and economic sustainability characteristics of acquaponic systems are only small-scale and therefore incur high costs of production relative to current methods of large-scale-farming.

However, in the future, due to human ought consider health, so who we need any food have good health quality to avoid any illness, e.g. cancer, even death causing risk from bad health foods source. In conclusion, food manufacturers need to consider any new food manufacturing methods to achieve how to manufacture foods to keep fresh and health level if they hope their food products can be attractive to consumers to choose to buy to eat.

Hence, future any new technological invention to manufacture health food will be one important factor to influence global food industry development. Also, it implies any food manufacturers need to consider how to manufacture any health foods in whose food manufacturing process. In conclusion, future foods and agriculture development will be trend to agriculture health productivity, avoidance from pests and diseases influence to food manufacturing process, avoidance food supply inequality and insecurity, more nutrition and health, changing food source manufacturing process system, reducing food losses and waste during food manufacturing process, making food systems more efficient, building resilience to protracted arises, disasters and conflicts, preventing transboundary and emerging agriculture and food system threats.

Future computer industry related service business strategy trends

● Government ( public) and private partnership property development strategy

In future some business, public and private partnership method is more suitable to compare the private entrepreneur sole operation. For example, property development, construction industry example, building and rebuilding cities and new communities is a complex challenge, it requires public and private interests and resources. However, the traditional process of urban and suburban can be developed between the local government and private property developer, which will win distinctly different benefits if they decide to cooperate together.

The need to rebuild and revitalize older portions of urban areas , the public need to monetize underused assets have dramatically changes. In fact, private sole property developer's disadvantages is that it has no longer can private capital be relied on to pay the high price of assembling and preparing appropriate sites for redevelopment. Also, it has no longer can local governments bear the full burden of paying the costs of public infrastructure and facilities. If public housing department and private property developer can cooperate to achieve shared goals and objectives, this process can require applying far more effort and skill to weighing, and then balancing, public and private interests and minimizing conflicts.

For another public and private partnership example, such as health care providers and education institutions, non profit associations, such as community based organizations and business improvement district organization , these organizations are very suitable to choose to cooperate with government ( public organization) to do their businesses together in the future global business environment trend.

However, the property development industry will have more benefits and needs to choose public and private partnership to compare these above industry. The main reason is that this industry will much capital to invest to any building business and it is long term tangible fixed property development business. Thus, the public and private property development partnership can implement a range of pursuits from projects to long term-plans for land use and economic growth. Partnerships have completed real estate projects, such as mixed-use developments, urban renewal through land and property assembly, public facilities, such as convention centers and airports and public services , such as affordable and military housing.

However, each public and private property development partnership is the best to share common stages with each development process as below:

In the first stage, conceptualization and initiation, stakeholders' opinions of the vision and surveyed and partners are selected through a competitive process.

In the second phase, entities document the partnership and begin to define project elements, roles and responsibilities, risks and rewards and the decision and implementation process.

In the third phase, the partnership attempts to obtain support from all stakeholders, including civil groups, local government ( through entitlement), and project team members.

Finally, in the fourth phase, the partnership begins construction, leasing and occupancy and property and asset management.

However, the process is repetitions and can continue beyond the final phase when partners manage properties or initiate new projects.

For US one successful public and private property development partnership example, the contributing major benefits to the citizens of Washington, D.C. The James Foyster School Henry Adams House, a public elementary school and 211 unit residential apartment complex was constructed as a result of a partnership among the District Of Columbia Public Schools.

● Online tourism service partnership

Another a major public and private partnership is tourism industry. Will public and private partnership to tourism be better than sole travel agent business operation? I believe it is better to any travel agent to choose public and private partnership strategy, the reasons include as below:

● Public tourism partnership goal, to provide the countries' different tourism destinations and tourism features to consider any country tourism information to assist travelers in understanding the travel problem, alternatives, opportunities and/or solutions to adapt every traveler individual travelling need.

● To obtain public travelling feedback on analysis, alternatives and/or travelling decisions, to work directly with the public throughout the travel public promotion process to ensure that public concerns and aspirations are consistent understood and considered, to partner with the public in each aspect of any tourism tickets comparison, tourism destinations, tourism entertainment, and transportation of the decision information , including the different tourism destinations development of alternatives and the identification of the preferred solution to place final decision -makings in the hands of the public.

● Every travel agent and public organization will keep every traveler's informed, listen and knowledge concerns and provide feedback on how public input influenced every tourism decision to every individual traveler considerately.

● Tourism techniques will consider fact sheet, web sites, open houses, public comment, focus tourism groups, surveys, public meetings, workshops, deliberate polling.

In conclusion, public and private partnership will be future trend to develop because capital can be shared, reduces sole business operation risks, promotes business information efficiently and easily when public organization can participate to assist these private business organization to cooperate to develop their businesses together.

● Higher education marketing, enrollment, branding and recruitment strategy

Future the most important tools for social and online education marketing will be an effective university website promotion tool to build ultimate brand for any university organization. Websites often feature elements and highlight content, including navigation, bars, engaging visuals, such as slideshows, and prominent " call to action" buttons that encourage students to apply. For example, radio ads., asking current students or for applicant referrals and online college fairs were deemed least effective, when the most effective methods of outreach open houses and campuses visit days for high school students.

Online education courses will be popular, due to adaptive learning technology has also enjoyed. So, successful branding can help increasing enrollment, expanding fundraising capabilities and other outcomes. Today, effective strategy planning and brand management require more than traditional advertising. Education institutions present and manage brand message, experience and environment achieve a competitive advantage in recruiting, building royalty among their students, parents , staff , faculty and donors.

In conclusion, how to do effective website advertising to promote university courses, website enrollment method? I shall recommend these methods as below:

Firstly, design responsive website, education institutions are placing more emphasis on responsive web design to create intuitive and easy to navigate websites that can be viewed on multiple, devices and platform.

Secondly, university administrators want their education institutions to receive a spot in search engine result particularly Google website. Especially for education institutions that offer niche programs , it is increasingly important to ensure that search results, including the programs at the top.

Thirdly, how to use of web analytics, colleges and universities are relying on data-driven analytic to determine who, whom and where they are reaching their audiences. The use of analytics software is increasing as the higher education web ecosystem is becoming complex, e.g. domains, subdomains etc.

Fourthly, getting a better handle of this data is a new area of concentration for colleges and universities strategic social media, when recent polls indicate nearly every education institutes of higher education use some form of social media, e.g. face book or twitter account, these trends are explored.

Fifthly, the rise of mobile development and connected decides to colleges and universities for a greater amount of course content of mobile versions of websites to promote to every student to know from whose every mobile, CRM systems are heavily on content management and customer relation systems for admission for prospective students service in the future mobile promotion technology.

Bibliography

Durmaz, Yaleup and Jablonski, Sabastian, ( 2012): Integrated Approach To Factors Affecting Consumers Purchase Behavior In Poland And An Empirical Study. Global Journal of management and business research ( GJMBR), volume 12 issue 15.

Ganesh, J., Arnold, M. and reynolds, K.E. ( 2000) ." Understanding The Customer Base Of Service Provides: An Examination Of The Differences Between Switchers And Stayers" , Journal of marketing, 64 (3), 65-88.

Journal of business and social science ( IJBSS). volume 2, no 5, p: 105110, radford USA. http://www.ijbssnet.com /journals/vol._2 _no._5 1 special_issue_March_2011J/13,pdf

Lamb, C.W. Hair, J. F. and Mc Daniel, C. (2011): " MKTD student edition". South Western , Mason.

Priest, J., Carter, S. And Stat , D. (2013) : Consumer Behavior, Edinburgh Business School Press, United Kingdom.


Further resources.

Reed Electronic Research, Yearbook Of World Electronic Data ( 2003)

Taiwan Minstry Of Economic Affairs ( 2003)

Internet market development trend


Nowadays , internet is a popular tool to be provided to human to apply, e.g. online commerce brings businessmen to do online business trading, online searching information brings anyone can find information in short time, online studying can brings online learning chance and none classroom attendance to students. However, if we often do any online behavior, it will influence our mental and physical health to be poor, e.g. often spending time to use internet for social media contact. This interactive technologies will influence every young people's brain, behavior and attitude to be poor because they often spend time to use computer at home. Then, this digital technologies will lead them to lack nervous to study or learn any new knowledge, when who are students if they often apply computer to learn and they do not need to contact classmates and teachers in classrooms. Consequently, their school examination results will be possible influenced to be bad if they often apply computer to learn because they do not spend other time to any recreational activities or contacting people to make friends activities in their daily life.

It brings these two questions:

(1) Will internet often be used use to influence young people's mental and physical health to be poor?

(2) Has it bring direct negative impact relationship when young people often spend time to use interest to do learning and information research behavior to cause poor mental and physical health?

Nowadays, human often uses internet which is one part of our habit. Our lives have become increasingly abuse in technology. Much of our communication and research is now online, much of our leisure and entertainment is provided by the internet and video games , and many of use internet find our mobile phones have become one essential part of our connectivity and everyday organizes to control our normal behaviors and to influence my normal life style poorly.

With these changes in lifestyle questions are it will arise negative influence about what technology may bring negative influence to us. Some of these questions bring potential detrimental effects, which had being unpredicted crisis in which the human brain is under threat from the modern world. Considerately, it influences the teenagers learning behaviors and attitudes to be poor. It seems that they have possible cause negative impact effect relationship between internet abuse habit behavior and poor mental and physical health as well as poor learning attitude and poor learning behaviors to young students.

The main factor of often doing internet playing behavior will have disadvantages to young people, because they will apply the internet tools to play video games to enjoy greater attention. This reflects a special case of environmental factor influence on whose mind and brain and health to be poor. Otherwise, if young people only spend some time to apply internet tools to do any reasonable need and meaning behavior, e.g. searching jobs from internet or searching any university written articles for study reference for learning intention or working seeking intention. Then, internet is a good tool to help them to develop their further career . Even, internet will train their brain and mind is more clear and clever and health to get advantages during who do any searching behavior for studying or learning intention from internet channel.

In conclusion, internet communication technology will bring either positive or negative influence to any users, it is depended on the user how to spend whose time to do any researching data or studying behavior in their daily time spending arrangement . Such as often playing game behavior or watching movie behavior and listening music entertainment behavior , which will have negative influence to any internet users' mind and physical health to be poor. Otherwise, sometimes searching jobs or seeking teaching articles or newspapers to read for learning intention from internet tool, which will have positive influence to any internet users. Hence, internet technology must not bring negative influence to human, it can also bring positive influence to human. It is depended on how we spend time to apply this high technology communication tools to do the beneficial mind and learning training behavior from this technological communication tool.

● How technology could contribute to bring poor standard of living to influence our societies

The effects of technology will have possible to bring global poor standard of living challenges. On the positive influence, especially science-based technology has offered a better world through the elimination of disease and material improvements to standards of living. But, on the negative influence, it will cause resource extraction, dangerous materials and pollution of air, water and oil have created conditions for unprecedented environmental to cause damage to the biosphere, when human applies any technologic tools to damage our earth natural environment in order to gain any profit for business aims.

Although technology brings businessmen to earn more profit, when who apply high technology to raise productivity and performance and efficiency to workers, e.g. artificial intelligence manufacturing robots, or they apply internet to sell their products (ecommerce), but technology also brings these disadvantages: Despite the ongoing technological revolution, the majority of the world population still lives in poverty with inadequate food, poor housing and less energy supply, illness increase , due to technological manufacturing can influence clean water and fresh air to be polluted to influence human's bodies to be un-health. Specially, the populations in Africa, Asia development countries, illness and death ratio both is risen by water and air pollution in these development countries nowadays.

Thus, it seems that it has relationship to bring negative influence to us between technology and air/water pollution and rising illnesses and deaths. Also, human needs to consider technology will support and enhance productivity and performance and efficiency , but it also influence human quality of standard to be poor challenge as the same time occurrence.

However, I suggest that businessmen ought reduce to invest much productivity by technological manufacturing improvement method, who ought concern environment pollution challenges how to avoid to apply technology to bring negative influence to all human's poor health challenge for long time. If human can apply technology, such as positive tool to solve problems or knowledge of how to create things, such as to brew beer , good

taste soft drink or fruit or to make an atomic bomb, and culture ( or understanding of the world, our value-systems), e.g. agriculture , irrigation and clean water management and navigation technological skill improvement. It means knowledge, technology becomes understanding of how to make and use tools and instruments becomes encodes as technological knowledge and know-how.

Consequently, human's positive and responsible behavior will change technology tools to develop of modern scientific knowledge, based on observations, hypotheses and generalizations on the natural laws concerning the behavior of materials and the living environment.

How to avoid to technology brings
negative influence on children

● Technology negative influence to children

In this world, it becomes impossible to escape the constant connection with others, aside from completely dis-connective from it, and into the unknown. Thus, parents need to know how their children using technological tools of behavior, which will influence impact on their children positively or negatively.

Nowadays, laptops and smartphones are now in the hands of children or young as ten age, and the eight to eighteen age young people that this group spends on average of ten hours and forty-five minutes or day exposed to media.

Whether their high amount of contact electronic media behavior is a good thing or not. So what is the right answer? Which side has the correct insight? When we may not have the immediate answer, one must look into both sides of the argument and determine what the correct path for today's children is. Thus, it brings thing effect, such as: one decision is about technology use will affect today's children as they develop.

Whether technology in classroom is truly a benefit for students. The benefits include it can enrich basic skills. Students who have access to technology become more quickly in the material and , such as are able to absorb the information more quickly. Electronic material can be more stimulating and interactive for children, it is motivational since it provides ease to students in study conducted of advanced learning technology students have found to have more interested to attempt to do writing behavior.

Nowadays, children can use technology as a supplement with traditional education, but it is as not replacement. In fact, computers have been specifically useful, for they allow us to manipulate items, such as text to meet the needs of individual students. For example, text can be made larger so it can be seen easier and also read aloud for deaf students. Moreover, recently, specific devices have been engineers to cater to students with specific disabilities. Thus, it seems that the introduction of technology into modern culture has drastically shifted social norms to include technology into children's daily lives.

However, when technology had been applied essentially into children's daily live. Technology also had bad points. Today, it is not uncommon to bring children playing on their portable video game systems, when at a restaurant with their family or to see a child operating a computer better than some adults. If children were abuse to use computer to video game wherever they go to any places, such as restaurant, school, toilet, catching transportation tool to sit down to play video games by mobiles habitually. It will bring this social challenge: Can technology influence children choose not to pursue to spend much time to learn, instead of often spending time to play video games for entertainment aim by mobiles habitually.

Technology will part of word of the rest of our foreseeable lives. But if children often accustomed to apply technology tool to play any video games from mobiles and internet tool. Consequently, they will often devote nervous and time to spend to play any video games from mobiles conveniently any time. Just like there have to be rules of conduct in real life, there have not to be smart rule of conduct in digital life to children.

The pursue of this internet and video games entertainment technology will force or encourage children to the playing video games from internet skills to navigate it and keep up with it as they get old. Hence, to judge electronic media is beneficial or harmful to children's learning stage . It is depended on how the child chooses to apply computer and/or internet technology from electronic media tool. If the child often use internet and computer or mobile tool to go to anywhere to concentrate on playing video games. Then, I believe that it will bring harm to the child's future learning development. Otherwise, if the child often use internet and computer or mobile tool to learn or seek any education articles in classroom or library or at home, these electronic tools are as technology advances to learn media. Then , it will be beneficial to the child's future learning development.

Technology negative influence to low knowledge learner to feel difficult to adopt future new technological labor market

Nowadays, information technology development is rapid. It brings this question: Will it bring negative influence to low knowledge learner to feel difficult to adopt future new technological labor market, special in underdevelopment of culture countries' labor markets?

To answer this question, firstly, we need to know what the underdevelopment of culture countries' labor market means before to answer this question. Culture means adaptive behavior, has been an integral feature of the human species through its evolution, it is shared, learned, symbolic, and transmitted cross generationally. In another sense, culture refers to all non-biological aspects of human existence, including economics, politics and technology. Underdevelopment of culture countries' labor market means what labors are needed to the under knowledge or educational level countries' labor markets.

There are very strong beliefs that the adoption and usage of information technology has performed positive effects on the development of any country, but it is not present that it will can bring negative effects on the underdevelopment of the culture countries, e.g. Africa, island places' living people, these places are not reactive or are not reaching technology mature stage. So, it brings these questions:

● What if the rate of adoption exceeds society's or individual's ability to adapt, when the rapid introduction of information technology?

● What if economic benefits are distributed in ways that are socially destabilizing?

● What if income distribution is unfair, with higher skilled personal becoming better compensated, when many people are deskilled and effectively unemployed of jobs comparable to their current jobs and at salaries comparable to what they are earning today?

● Can their low knowledgeable workers feel difficult to learn any high technological skill to prepare their future job demand in these underdevelopment countries?

It seems rapid information technology to underdevelopment culture countries , which have chances to cause social challenges. Such as low skilled workers' unemployment , even office workers' salaries or technology manufacturing factory workers' wages will be reduced if who would not adapt the new technology development to follow the new technology influence to impact their work culture or method.

Thus, it also seems that culture can't exist without some form of society, i.e. culture us social. Therefore, cultural factors are observed in the society as providing to the production of its members who need to apply technological tools to manufacture products or serve their clients in their job responsibilities, e.g. factory workers, restaurant waiters etc. low skilled and learned workers. They need to learn how to apply new technology to work, e.g. computer skill or artificial intelligent skill.

So, it explains why rapid technology development will influence the low culture under development countries' low knowledge and low skillful workers to feel difficult to adapt how to learn to apply new technology production in themselves countries' technological job nature development change . Then , it will cause social challenges, such as unemployment, reducing wages, dismiss them, raising domestic labor market competition.

Moreover, some scientists concerned with the negative labor competition impact effect of information technology on the underdevelopment countries' low knowledgeable level of workers rather than the economic contribution of IT, because when many low knowledgeable level of workers feel difficult to learn technological skill to do their jobs, then they will be dismissed possible to bring social unemployment number to be increased and shortage of labor in these underdevelopment culture countries . In essence, they was asking if IT would erode this unique possession , even if it seems to contribute to their economic development.

Consequently, the intensive use of computer by the low knowledgeable skillful labors before the realization of whose thought –high technological production method itself may prevent the low knowledgeable workers' productive form being able to develop as a creatively thinking personally. This is a negative example of a mental process to them, which has been defined earlier.

In conclusion, the development of a new information society to under development culture countries would then raise a number of fundamental problems, one of which could be how to formulate and create optional cognitive preconditions for successful low knowledgeable labor' upgrade of high technological skill in short term. There are some pf the problems faced by developing nations who are still to development their technological production skill to low knowledgeable workers to let them feel difficult properly, let alone creating optimal preconditions for a successful mental process of low knowledge labor-computer interaction. At present, the adoption of IT in developing counties needed to be concern how to adapt whose countries' information technological labor users' production skill change.

The negative impact of smartphones/ mobiles and
desktop/ laptop on human health and life

● Avoidance to driving and speaking mobile at the same time

Nowadays, the smartphones being a very new invention of humanity, became an inherent part of human's life. The smartphone combines different features. It allows users to keep pictures, memories, personal information correspondence, health and financial data in one place. Smartphones also become an integral part of modern telecommunications facilities. In some regions of the world, they are the most reliable only of available places. The phones allow people to maintain continuous communication without interruption of their movement and distances. However, recent scientific facts and research analysis of the smartphones' usage has disadvantages to influence human health and life.

The main key points indicate the effect of electromagnetic waves on human brains, effect of handheld device usage on human's upper extremities, back and neck. A significant neglect influence between the total time spend using mobile device each day and pain in the right shoulder and between times spent internet browsing and pain at the base of the right thumb. Moreover, mass cellphone calls enhance risk to human safety, e.g. when they are driving and listening and talking to touch mobiles at the same time. The drivers' driving and phoning calls behavior at the same time which will be very dangerous of their speaking and driving to cause traffic accident occurrence in possible. Thus, drivers can not neglect to avoid to do the mobile speaking and driving behavior at the same time when they are driving to reduce their traffic accident occurrence to cause their death or hurt in possible.

● What are the negative effect of electromagnetic waves on human brains from smartphone influence

Scientists proved that the smartphone is a source of the eminence of electromagnetic waves. Numerous studies have been conducted in the past years to identify the effect of electromagnetic waves emitted from the cell phones on human health.

However, it has not proved smartphone can influence our health certainly. As soon as mobile phones more and more part of our lives, the world is continuing research to prove whether cell phones are harmful to human health.

Today, there is no official statement announced by laboratory or medical center to answer this question: The complexity of the analysis of the statistical data makes the task more difficult for researchers. The impact of harmful radiation emitted from cell phones is still being studies.

Nowadays, human are accepted to use mobile phone in any time, any where popularly. Although, mobile is a good small size and convenient carrying of communication tool for human to use when we need to make phone calls to anyone in anywhere and any time conveniently. But, I feel that it will harm human health when we often use this communication tool any time.

However, some doctors indicate cell phones can cause brain cancer risk easily. But they have not any evidences to prove it is truth nowadays. Hence, the statement that cell phones can cause cancer has been not confirmed. The studies failed to prove that cellphones make a major risk develop cancer among frequent users. The main issues when conducting studies are some people may not accurately report the usage as they don't exactly remember how often they use the cell phone excluding speaker phone , and it is still difficult to measure the impact of other factors that may accelerate the cancer development for excessive cell phone users.

Although, it is not proved that cellphone can use brain cancer to human when we often use. But some scientists or medical professionals have proved that the cell phone users often use cell phones , it is possible to cause human physical illnesses, such as upper extremities, back and neck caused unhealthy and pain.

A smartphone or handhelds device combines advanced computing capability, such as internet communication, information retrieval, video, e-commerce and other features, that make device highly popular among people. According to Pew research center investigating, it showed that the number of smartphone owners comprises 56% of American adults in 2013 year and their average daily use of the device is about 195 minutes. The number of cellphone users increase every year. Various studies show the connection between cellphones usage and physical illness of the users' health. Some studies report that users complain about a headache, hand tremor and finger discomfort and pain of physical illnesses numbers increasing.

In fact, most mobile hand-held device users complain of discomfort at least on one area of upper extremities, back or neck. Long –term usage of the device leads to additional tension on tenders , muscles and tissue etc. different kind of physical illnesses. Moreover, in research conducted by a group of Korean scientists from Inji University focused that an effect of cellphone on hand-held device users was a significant association between the total time spend using a mobile device each day and pain in the right shoulder, and between times spend internet browsing and pain at the base of the right thumb.

● The laptop and desktop negative influence

On the laptop and desktop negative influence aspect, although telecommuting and telework communication technology is popular to be applied to our daily life. For example, they are modern alternative to office arrangement, employees work from home office, café, garden, carpark , even car.

According to scientists showed that nowadays, there are 20 to 30 million people who work from their home at least one day each week. Another 15 to 20 million work when they are on the road, 10 to 20 million runs some form of home business and 15 to 20 million work at home part of the time. IN most cases, people use desktop and laptop in their home office.

However, modified cellphones or smartphones are also substitutes to a home office. In fact, in principle of computers, it makes the workplace safer and convenient to compare mobile phones. There are different examples of adaption desktop or laptop computers to health needs of these users when bring their computers to go to anywhere to use in common, e.g. ergonomically designed keyboards design, pad bolster, mouse etc. design to adapt to their carrying to use their laptop or desktop needs. However, laptop or desktop computer products have not proved any serious harmful to influence human health to compare mobile phones at this moment.

Consequently , although technology can create different kind of jobs to let human to do, or assist human to communicate conveniently, e.g. mobile or artificial intelligent robot assist human to do any clerical job duties or learning more easily, .e.g. internet or laptop or desktop or owning mobile and laptop function computer products. There high technological products can bring benefits to satisfy human needs, .e.g. raising productivity efficiencies for workers, providing far distance overseas phone calls telecommunication, searching data or electronic business running from internet channel. But human can not neglect that these high technological products whether will bring negative influence to our mental or physical health when we often use them in possible. Thus, often using high technologies products to influence our health issue will be one important matter to be our future consideration.

Future internet function development trend
● Online television
Online television channels, platforms, devices experiences and choice will be positioning entertainment consumer market for the foreseeabl future. The reason is onlin ebook, music entertainment has been popular. Why does online television won't be popular?
Bloomberg business week website (2013) indicated that the evaluation of control technological development of portability technological tool: from 1975 year , the astraltune product had been populaar. The, 1979 year, Sony walkman had reached the 200 million sold number. Next, 1994 year, the smartphone had reached 1.4 billion users. Following 2001 year, the Apple ipod had reached 350 million sold. Then, 2010 year, the Apple ipod had reached 100 million sold. However, in watching television/movie entertainment consumption consumers could have different choice, e.g. from 1975 year, consumers can choose VCR entertainment tapes to watch movies or television programs. Then, from 1995 year, consumers can choose DVD , following from 2007 year consumers can choose Netflix streaming recording cameras to record any movies or television programs to watch. It had reached 30 million subscription numbers. Following from 2012 year, entertainment consumers can choose Acreo FM internet signal to watch TV.
Anyway, the entertainment watching facilities development had been following this trend: Capacity from 1981 year, the capacity is broadband. then, from 1999 year, capacity is WiFi, it had 61% of households share

market. Next, from 2001 year, the capacity is 3G technology, many people like to download any movies or TV programes to mobile phone to watch. Till to nowadays, the mobile phone capacity is improved to 4G technology, the mobile phone internet user number had reached 59 million current subscribers. So, it implies that many entertainment consumers like to use internet to download any movies or TV programs to mobile phones or laptops to watch.

It implies future internet development trend which can be used to entertainment industry. Hence, the future of television ought have implications for the component of a media company, when it applies internet technology to operate, such as IT service management, disaster recovery, digital content security, cloud etc. technological development.

Interactive advertising bureau (2013) indicated the devices used to view online television among US digital video viewers by type Mar 2013 1% of respondent(s), laptp had 58%, internet-connected TV had 47%, desktop has 39%, smartphone had 28%, tablet had 28% , ipodtouch had 14%.

Hence, it implied many entertainment consumers prefer to use laptop or internet connected to watch online TV television or movie in the future. These two channels will be the most popular online TV/movie entertainment channels in the future. Moreover, future internet technology development ought concentrate on improving it's speed, quality, performance to satisfy any laptop or internet connect TV entertainment consumers. Hence, future internet technology development ought concentrate on improving it's speed, quality, performance to satisfy any laptop or internet connect TV entertainment consumers.

● Internet innovative logistic industry

What is future potential benefits and limitations of using internet to logistic operaters? The users pay attention to two new developments that may have a very large impact on the development of logistic has been pointed out, i.e. To the " internet of everything" and to the so-called fourth industrial revolution. Will internet be popular used by logistic transportation industry?

Nowadays, logistic transportation industry is facing challenges, factors include possibly quickest onset of transportation action, high efficiency as well as flexibility, whose main function is the maximinal adaptation to client needs, e.g. delivering any products or documents to any countries' clients in the most time and no any error to deliver the products or documents to the wrong receivers.

However, internet is increasingly influenced by the skillful management of modern technologies to assist delivering in efficiency. It is based on complex and comprehensive data sources, arising from and influencing the development of modern trends. So, logistic industry needs have internet technology to help modern production, processing and logistics processes to satisfy the expectations of stakeholders.

The internet of things ( IOT) is a new modes of communication, information connection between people and things, but in particular connection between objects ( things). Hence, IOT management systems have a very wide range of applications and in terms of logistics, in a direct or in direct way many cover, among other, smart cities, intelligent industry, intelligent enterprises, intelligent buildings.

In the future, the group of significant trends in logistics include: big data/ open data, cloud logistics; autonomous logistics, 3D printing, robotics and automation; internet of things; localization and local intelligence; wearable technology;augmented reality; low-cost sensor technology; crypto-currencies and crypto-payment. Hence, future logistics industry will need internet technology assistance to develop any businesses. For example, DHL logistic delivering firm, the first 6 trends belong to a group that will impact on : Firstly, big data/open data, it is a degree of digitization enterprise data can be shared in an unprecedented way. Integrated data streams in the supply chain of many logistic suppliers and open data sources have a very high potential for logistics operations, improvement of operational efficiency, full control over the suppl chain, assets and personal , the possibility of more accurate forecasts, and adjustment in real time.

Secondly, what is cloud logistics? It meets the challenges of complex diistributed , uncertains less predictable logistic conditions, reduction of the total cost of IT services ( including the cost of installation, updatin , maintenance fees)., service risk minimization, faster and simply implementation, better reliability and security.

Thirdly, automonus logistic: It is stand-alone devices can be applied throughout. The supply chain from " the warehouse of the future" through auto-driven vehicles. Following the example of autopilots to unmanned supplies.

Fourthly, 3D printing is technology chnging the logistics by adding new manufacturing " mthods and possibl emergence of new market segments, such as the digital magazone.

Firthly, robotics and automation is the new generation of robots and automated solution will significantly better performance offers a serious alternative to manual labor, reducing time consuming actitivied aim. So, these will be internet is how applied to logistics industry trend in the future.

● Six key forces or " Drivers of change" impact on future internet development

In the future, there will have to key drivers of change impact on future internet development, it includes : the internet and the physical world, artificial intelligence, cyber threats, the internet economy, networks, standards and interoperability and role of government. However, thesedrivers will have three areas of impact include: digital divides, personal freedoms and rights and media and society.

However, future internet technology will have these threats to influence its development. They include: civil society is seen as more important to raise needs, internet must remain user centric to raise competition, it is critical for individual safety and for the future internet economy, new thinking , new approaches and new models are needed across the board from internet policy to addressing digital divides from security approaches to economic regulation, multi-stakeholder needs will change increasing frequenty, internet users wil consider data collection and privacy in confidence.

In the future, artifical intelligent development will incresse internet needs in possible. The advent of artificial intelligence (AI) promises new opportunities, ranging from new services and breakthroughs in science to the augmentation of human intelligence in digitial world. For example, when there is significant hype about the possibilities hat (AI) may bring voices of concern to apply internet technology assistance. Hence, human must ensure that humans remain in the " internet and (AI) driver's technology combination ."

Consequently, the hyperconnected internet economy that results will see traditionl industries to lead future new internet market leaders from around the globl driving innovation and entreprensurship. Hence, future internet and (AI) will be technological driven economy, it depends on how scientists improve their innovation.

However, scientists ethical consideration will be one important issue when they decide how to apply internet and (AI) technology. If they choose to apply them to war aspect, it is very horror matter to human's future safety. Hence, developing (AI) and internet technological countries need to consider scientist's behaviors in order to avoid war occurrence to cause human's death in future one day.

Hence, scientists ought follow this direction to develop internet technology. The future internet is needed to promise social development , economic prosperity and technologies that can ampify the best of humanity. But, it also brings about to solve challenges and questions to achieve to aim to raise human's social welfare or beneficial final direction.

What will be the certain factors to shape the future of the internet development? It includes as below: Social economic opportunity factor, it refers this ability how to connect people is essential to the internet's value as a platform for innovation, creativity and economic opportunity. How can the drivers of change encompass internet technological , economic, regulatory, security and network related challenges for the future internet . The drivers of change may include, such as how the internet economy development, what the role of government is, what the internet and physical world will shape, how internet assists artificial intelligent development, how to fight cyber threats, how networks standards and interoperable developments.

Future hospital, transportation, manufacturing etc. industries development factor how these industries develop, it will influence how internet needs. Because the rapid change will disrupt businesses and increse pressure on societies , particularly models and the nature of work will be profoundly changed to influence internet change needs. It is far from clear whether this internet technology driven assistance will favour existing internet platforms or bring greater competition and internet entrepreneurship.

How the internet economy will increase efficiencies, productivity and create new opportunities factor. Internet technology will reshape economies in ways stakeholders, and particularly governments may be ill-equipped to keep up with. And as technology drives automation, traditional jobs and the local economies that rely on them will be at risk. So, the future internet economy will depend on new approaches to skills and education. For example, traditional manufacturing sectors that were once relatively insulated must evolve to succeed in an increasingly connected internet economy. As devices and applicances are built to be network ready, the internet live needs us between manufacturing and manufacturing technological company increasing. Companies will need to adopt a technology mindset as they are from replacing parts to updating software to manufacture efficiently by internet and artificial intelligent technology assistance. Also, business is trying to protect against disruptions to their business models, for example, in the tussle between Google's automated cars and the automobile industry. For one, it's another application of sensor technology for the other , it's a change in mindset.

In the future, most widely used online services and platforms deeped their market position or face competition and possible displacement by new players? Could these internet companies face new competition from traditional industries as online in a world of IOT? Can internet platform be popular to be used for advertisements for businesses? (AI)/new generation of entrepreneurs like to use technology to solve local problems, reach global markets and drive innovation. Hence, online ( internet ) data search can be the best tool to help them to achieve their intention. I believe that it has not other technology can be replace internet to search lot of data in the short time within 10 years. Hence, internet of things ( IOT) ought follo this direction to improve its quality to attract many clients. ( entrepreneurs) to use this data serch service.

Moreover, artificial intelligence will be popular to be used. It will be beneficial to internet to be used. For example, a society completely based on data collection on the business. Humans lose some self-determination through automated choices by connected machines. So, our community across all stakeholder groups and regions believes that automation generated through data analytics technology will have greater influence on human behavior and decision making. So (AI) and internet can be cooperate to assist themselves to serve human. For example, (AI) could bring about a fundmental reshaping of decision-making as policy development's increasingly data driven. AS (AI) and automation drive significant structural change across industries, the nature of work will change. Many existing jobs may be displaced as (AI) moves beyond user data to changing how products and services are delivered from internet assistance. The communication between machine to machine increases pressures to cut costs and people are being replaced. This is only going to increase with time. There are economic benefits , but also challenges to employees.

Hence, if the internet platforms of today can become dominant across infrastructure, services and applications, user choice and control over their online experience, as well as availability and deliversity of information and content could be popular factor to influence internet economy. When search companies reach such a level of scalability, it is difficult for others to complete with them. For example, customers may find it is difficult to move from one provider or platform to another. This will cause in the loss of choice and constraints on innovation and lead to internet fragmentation. This is a trend to toward an ecosystem of users and developers, in which you can have the big winners or something similar to walled gardens. But there will always be some disruption tahta fragments this garden and creates a new paradigm. So , the reach and resources of internet platforms mean that startups will be acquired in their infancy, before they can disrupt the bigger players.

Will any internet companies replace Google, yahoo internet companies' services? This question is if smaller entrepreneurs are able to compare in an able to compete in an uncertain environment of investment analysis to the opportunities, these creates are ranging from new big data search service to the applied to intelligence in the digital world. So, artificial intelligence will be creative destruction. Many jobs will be also be eliminated by (AI) technological invention, but it can generate new jobs and jobs from internet , big data serch services assistance.

● Future trend of mobile and internet development

Morgn Stanley reserch indicated that future past mobile vs. desttop internet user development trend within 5 years. Mobile internet users number was from 400 million 2007 year climbed up to 1,900 million 2015 year. Otherwise, desktop internet users number was from 1,000 millon 2007 year climbed up to 1,7500 million 2015 year. Hence, it implied that , although desktop internet user number was more than mobile internet user number in 2007 yer, but till to 2015 year,mobile internet user number was more than desktop internet user number. It reflect many people had accepted to apply mobile tool to do any internet search behaviors. It is possible that it will be popular to apply mobile tool to do internet search behaviors for long time in the future.

It brings this interesting question: Why do global internet users prefer to spend more time to apply mobile tools to do search behaviors from internet? I shall indicate that this technological teaching method example, such as how smart mobile phones and internet technolgy had changed the old phenomena of learning model in educational industry. The traditional phenomena of learning model was that teaching innovation means unit cost of teaching, success teaching evidence means number of teaching units deployed, every student can free access open teaching contents from internet channel of desktop tools, every student learning can be achieved every delivery and display from internet learning, every teacher training needs to achieve the first and last discussion to every student from internet online teaching tool. Hence, many schools will accept to teach students from online teaching channel. Every student can turn on desktop to link to internet tool to learn at home conveniently. So, internet learning students do not need to go to schools, due to internet learning tool is similar to classroom to let teachers can apply internet channel to teach their students as well as students can listen their one teacher teach what in the same time when they open computer to link internet to see their teacher face and listen what who teach them after they log in their school website from internet channel conveniently. Hence, every group of students who can see teacher and listen what their teacher is teaching them in the same time after they turn on desktop to link to internet at home.

Some scientists also predict future mobie internet can be applied in educational and communication industries from 2020 year. Mobile internet can be applied to these aspects: education security, labguages, radio distributed systems, networking.

How can mobile internet be applied to children age education industry? I shall explain what what pocket school means. Pocketschool is not a name of device to be applied to different device for a different context, it is not a name software varies of open software contents, it is an initiative to help underrepresented children and migitate digital, education and economic divides. For a kind of mobile math learning game education method, it is a critical thinking math teaching method to children. Every child student can turn on mobile to learn how to apply simply math equation to calculation from mobile internet. Hence, future mobile internet tool won't only be applied to playing game aspect, it can be applied on education game aspect to let children to feel fun to learn from themselves. So, children can apply mobile internet to learn from device recognition to solve problem through collaborations, e.g. children cn apply moile internet tool to learn writting story ot telling story to increase learning internet or training to be authors. Mobile internet can also be applied to medical aspect, e.g. seeing any x ray images of brains , bones or any part of bodies, when medical photographs are delivered to download to the patient's mobile from the hospital easily.

In conclusion, in the future mobile internet will be popular used by mobile users and internet market must be expand to mobile tool market, instead of computer tool market.

● Digital Pollution prediction tool development

Can internet (digital) technology be fueled by the social, mobile, cloud, big data gathering and growing demand for anytime, anywhere access to information to help scientists to predict when or why or how any natural environment bad climate change occurrence and find any solutions to avoid any pollution is caused which can reach the serious level by human's damage natural environment behaviors?

Nowadays, the evolution of digital tool development, human can apply this tool to gather big data to help any businesses to decide to best activity to reduce loss, or to analyze information to get the more accurate result. In the future, I believe that digital technology can be applied to help scientist to gather nature climate and environment change data to analyze when the climate will be changed to be worse. Even, when water and /or air and/or soil and/or noise different kinds of pollution will be serious to influence the country's people's health, e.g. water is polluted to drink or air is polluted to breathe or soil is polluted to grow food or noise is serious to influence our mental health. Even, digital big data can help scientists to find the reasons why the country's air and/or water and/or soil and/or noise pollution is caused and attempt to find any solutions more accurate to avoid the serious level of any pollution occurrence.

Moreover, in the micro –economic benefits, digital tool will develop to be used to predict the level of water/air/soil/noise pollution to assist policy decision makers to do any effective policies to response to these nature climate change challenges that cities face, include climate change and poverty, will be essential to making cities of the future competition.

Thus, digital technology seems to be future one kind of the most suitable climate change or environment pollution big data gathering predict tool to compare other climate change predict technological tools.

● Future digital technology prediction tool development trend

Nowadays, cloud, big data demand is growing to be satisfy to any different businesses or personal needs. In the future, it seems to be applied to help scientists to attempt to gather any big data to save to cloud ( internet saving channel) , to analyze why ,when, how to cause the water/air/soil/ noise pollution will reach the serious level and , to find the best solution to solve the causes of any pollutions accurately.

Digital technology will be one good prediction tool to help scientists, even who are not scientists to gather data to do any analyses concern climate change or environment pollution easily. It's advantage is any people who do not need to spend more time to learn and feel difficult to learn how to apply this technological tool to compare other difficult learning of technological climate prediction tools generally. Since, internet (digital) is one kind of popular and cheap technological product to be used, any people can free change to use it when who are using in public library , school library, any transportation tools, such as bus, ferry, tram, train, taxi private cars, or restaurant, shopping centers etc. different public places. Hence, gathering data activities are very convenient and easily to any people and it is one good prediction to predict when ,how, why natural environment change and climate change and pollution causes when people can bring whose laptops to go to anywhere to apply internet (digital) tool to gather any climate and environment data change immediately.

# CHAPTER FIVE

# Airport indoor travelling staying shopping market

Emotional labor factor

Airline service industry, front line travelling passengers service workers' emotional challenge concerns cabin crew and airline ground service employee whose service quality or performance how to serve travelling passengers in order to reach service level or satisfy their service performance needs to be accepted. So, how to influence airline service labour individual emotional matter which will be one major factor to let travelling passengers how they feel satisfactory to the airline service.

The question concerns how to let airline service cabin crews and air ground service employees build long term good emotion to serve their airline travelling passengers. Because
bad emotional airline service labors will damage the whole airline employers' loyalty as well as reducing travelling passengers number in possible.

Will a lot stresses at work cause bad emotion to airline ground service employees? The hospitality industry comprises of travel and tourism and the major segments include lodgings and cuisines ( hotels, restaurants), transport( airlines, rentals, cruise and railway companies), travel and tour operators. All of these related travelling industries' employees , they are emotional labor, whose service performance or service attitude will influence future potential travelling passengers' airline choices to the airline operating servicer again. Any airline service employees in these service sector industries, have to interact with their travelling clients, be its customers on a regular emotion reflecting basis. So, they must be patient to listen any travelling passengers' enquires in order to help them to solve any problems considerably.

Emotional labor is managing one's feelings to generate a publicly accepted facial and bodily display of emotion. Emotional labor is an expression of emotion for a wage. Jobs involve face to face or voice to voice interactions with clients ( travelling passengers), jobs demanding the employee to produce and alter an emotional state in other person, and jobs allowing the employer to implement certain amount of control over the emotional activities of the employees, produce or create emotional labor among the employees.

Thus, long time bad emotional airline front labors number increasing, it will influence the airline whole service member performance to be its airline passengers. However, many airline organizations have their owning set of norms or policies that determine these feeling rules. These are specially seen in customer service industries. IN long term, these strict policies will let airline front service staffs feel stress or pressure, because they won't feel to be punished in possible, e.g. without salary continue increasing, dismissal ( lose jobs), changing to another position to do more simple or boring job duties, if they are discovered that their working service performances are not satisfied to their airline employers in any time.

So, strict airline organizational policies will be one strict or pressure emotional regulation to any airline front service staffs. This emotional regulation refers to a person's capability to accept and understand his or her experience of emotions to get involved in healthy strategies in managing emotions which are uncomfortable whenever required, when they need to contact their airline passengers every day. In fact, it has possible that they will accept unreasonable complaint from their airline passengers, even they perform very good or they have help their airline passengers to solve any enquiries when they feel any needs, they stay in airports any time. So, it has close relationship among airline front service staffs' emotions and the airline's policy as well as their service attitude. Thus, good airline policy will build good airline service staffs' emotions and good service attitude or service behaviour to serve their airline passengers every day in possible.

Any airline organizations can not neglect to consider how to build (keep) good airline front labor emotion issue. Because they are any airlines' representatives, if they can build good

images to let the airline the airline passengers to feel. Then, it will influence many airline passengers to choose to buy the airline tickets to replace other airlines because they like its front airline front staffs' services. SO, any airline organizations need to consider front service staffs' health status and definite psychological or mental diseases more than physical diseases, because many airline front service staffs only need to serve their airline passengers and they do not need to move any heavy things in airports in general. They need to spend more time to contract their passengers more than any things. When their passengers give their passports or/and any related travelling documents, e.g. air tickets to them to check in to find whether they can allow to enter airport restrict areas, and if they give their luggage to them, they also need to help them to measure its size and weight heavy to decide whether they need to pay extra fee and their luggage are permitted either to keep to them together to enter the air planes to fly or separate air planes to fly to destination. So, they need to make accurate judgement need to avoid any error occurrence. They do not allow to do any wrong judgement or error in order to be complain by their airline passengers often. Hence, any airline organizations need have good method to help their airline front service staffs to avoid to do any wrong judgements in order to influence any flights delay or customers' complaints , due to their personal wrong judgement to their passengers cause in possible.

Thus, any airline organizations require to enquire themselves these questions: Is there any influence of emotional labor ( surface acting and deep acting) on the general mental health or psychological disease of airline employees? Is these any difference in the experience of emotional labor across demographics ( age/gender/mental status/work experience of airline employees influence their service performance? Because above any one factors , such as every airline front service staff individual age, airline service experience, marital status of these factors will influence their emotions to be good or bad to serve their airline passengers every day. Hence , any airline organizations need to investigate every airline front service employee individual background in order to arrange the most suitable policy to train their front line or ground airline service staffs' skill in order to let them to feel less stress or pressure
or they can feel happy to enjoy to serve their airline passengers.

On conclusion, reducing airline front or ground service staffs' psychological stress or mental pressure issue which will be the most effective or the best solution to assist them to raise confidence to serve their airline passengers in airports in long time. I believe that it is the most rapid psychological solution method to assist any one airline front or ground service staff to raise service level in short time.

Airports service environment factor

The environment of airports service environment for the airline services, which will also influence travelling passengers' travelling destinations and travelling frequent times choices. The airport price factor includes income growth, aviation technology and local economic / geographical features of the country's domestic or overseas airports both. IN fact, airports, airports are indeed two sides businesses, it has commercial relationship between both airlines and passengers. So, airports' pricing will influence passengers' travelling demands to the airlines in the country. Any countries' airport(s) need(s) to respond how to help themselves country airlines how to increase passengers number and airlines choices in order to achieve attracting traffic on frequent air planes flying aim. Because the country's travelling passengers number increases , it will influence the country's airport(s) ' income increases indirectly, instead of the countries' any airlines themselves incomes.

Hence, any country's airport(s) will be one good platform to let travelling passengers to stay in the country's airport(s). It means that id the country's airport(s) can build good service image and reasonable products sale price and comfortable shopping environment to attract any countries' passengers feel comfortable and worth to stay in themselves countries' airport(s), when they need to transfer air planes to stay in the country's airport, e.g. one hour to five hours short time, even overnight long time staying. However, if they
feel the country's airport(s) are(is) more comfortable and clean to stay, less noise, as well as they have enough chairs to let them to sit or sleep and large area to let them to work in the airport ground floor.

Moreover, the country's airport(s) can have enough restaurants , bookshops, any electronic or other kinds product shop[s, even cinema etc. shopping or entertainment services to satisfy
the passengers whose eating needs, entertainment needs, shopping needs in the airport. Then, I believe that the country's airport(s) can help itself airlines to attract many passengers
to choose to increase travelling times to the country frequently. For example, when the country's airport passengers feel that the airport restaurant food concessionaires will probably provide enjoy positive external gains from having more flights at the airports, additional or better eating facilities are unlikely to provide external benefits to the airlines by stimulating many more passengers with local origins or destinations to use

the airport. I believe these airport restaurants can influence the choices of transit passengers whether which country will be their transfer air plane's short journey staying airport destination to fly to their final destinations. Although, transit passengers usually stay to the transfer air plane airport in short time, but they hope that these any one transit staying airport can have any restaurants to provide good taste food to them to eat when they feel hungry, if the transfer air plane country's airport can provide enough restaurants and they can have different food taste choice and reasonable price. Then, the airport's restaurants may attract many short time transit passengers to choose to eat their food, even many passengers will like to choose the country's airline to buy tickets to stay short time to wait to transfer another air plane to fly to their final destination to replace another country's airport to stay short time.

Hence, it seems that any countries' airports' entertainment, eating and shopping service environment will influence any countries transit passengers whether they ought either choose to stay short time this country's airport in prefer or another country's airport to stay short time in prefer in order to decide to buy the country's airline air ticket for transfer airplane to another destination. Hence, any airports service environment will influence any countries passengers how to make transit airport destination short time staying choice.

However, I also suggest that an airport will place a lower revenue -over cost burden on that side of the travelling market that benefits the other the most. Assuming one passenger
can earn benefit enjoyed by airlines from an extra- passenger using the airport, the airlines will be willing to pay up to this amount to increase passenger enjoyed benefit feeling.

The airport can extract rent from the airlines up to above their allocated costs for providing the airport short time staying platform ( transfer air plane short time staying airport ) for eating, entertainment, shopping need service of increasing their destination arriving passengers or transfer another air plane passengers number base. This involves transferring the external benefits derived by airlines from additional passengers using the transfer airport to the another destination airport.

On the another view, from a airport location choice perspective, locating or expanding an airport near a city center can reduce or at least contain passenger access costs . But, because land is
like to be more expensive, the airside costs to airlines are serious higher

and if the various other external costs of aviation are included. Hence, countryside or the airport is built far away from city center in the country. This location is one reasonable location choice, because it can reduce noise to influence people who are living when air planes are often flying or landing on the airport and the rent cost to the airport's any business renters will be influenced to reduce. Then, their food , product or entertainment service prices charge to the airport consumers will also be reduced. Thus, any airports ought nor neglect their building location choices in any countries because they will influence airport business renters sale prices.

Lean maintenance repair and manual
error factor

Any airlines must need air plans to catch passengers to fly to travel. So, any air plans will need often to fly. Every flight will need long time to fly, e.g. short trip needs to fly less than five hours, even long trip needs to fly more than five hours, even ten hours. If many passengers choose the country to travel, the air plan needs to fly
frequently to catch every flight passengers to go to the travelling destination frequently. So, any airlines air plans often need to check whether they have any engine machines has broken, need to be repaired in possible in order to let passengers feel the airline air plans are safe. If the airline's any air plans have occurred any accidents when they are flying, even the accidents cause any one passengers hurt, even death. Then, these flying accidents will let passengers feel life risk to choose this airline's any air plans to catch to fly. IN special, long time trip(s) flight(s). So, lean maintenance and engine check is needed to consider for any one airplane to any airline in order to improve efficiencies and minimize costs, maintenance, repair,
and overhaul services in the aviation industry sector, even avoiding any flying accident occurrence or reducing serious flying accidents occurrence chance to bring any one passenger
hurt, even death when they are catching any one of the airline air plans to travel. Thus, any one of airline safety is one important successful factor to any airlines.

Instead of passenger safety aspect, the flying logistics safety factor is also important. The central tenet of the lean to a flying process can mainfest in a variety of ways , as over stalled
and underused inventory and misallocated labour, time transportation and logistics. From a customer's perspective, value-added activities are

necessary and customers are willing to pay for activities(Bamber, 2000, Glass, 2016). For example, improvements caused by lean introduction in aviation industry in order to avoid misallocated labour time, increasing number of old broken tools, and obsolute jigs and fixtures. Aviation MRO services have been reported by the MIT Lean Aerospace Initiative (2005) to result in:

(1) Set up time: 17 to 85 percent improvement.

(2) Lead time: 16 to 50 percent improvement.

(3) Labour hours: 10 to 71 percent improvement.

(4) Cost: 11 to 50 percent improvement.

(5) Productivity: 27 to 100 percent improvement.

(6) Cycle time: 20 to 97 percent improvement.

(7) Airline airplane manufacturing factory floor space: 25 to 81 percent improvement.

(8) Travel distance ( people and products): 42 to 95 percent improvement.

(9) Airplanes engine inventory or work in progress: 31 to 98 percent improvement.

(10) Scape, rework , deflects or inspection: 20 to 80 percent improvement.

Hence, any airlines' airplanes need to be achieve any one of above improvement at least percent level in order to keep airplane's accident occurrence chance to the least level.

Moreover, airplanes' pilot employees their flying experiences or flight numbers factor is also important to influence airplane safe flying issue. Because if the pilot has less flying

expereince or he is not proficient pilot, or his flight number is less. This pilot's individual flying factor will also influence the airplan's safety when he is driving the airplane.

So, any airlines need to consider how to train any one of pilot to be one proficient pilot, because id less experienced pilot , he/she is not proficient to drive any one airplane to fly. Then, the flying accident occurrence chance will also raise. It is one critical successful factor to influence passengers' confidence to choose the airline's airplanes to catch, instead of maintenance repair and checking engines factor.

On conclusion, raising travelling passengers' safe confidences factor will be one critical successful factor to influence any airlines' services level, because flying safety issue

must be one important matter to be considered to any passengers when they decide to choose the airline's airplane to catch to fly to any destinations. If one airline can not guarantee any flying accidents won't occur, to cause any passengers hurt or death. Then, any passengers won't have confidence to feel its others services level can satisfy their basic flying enjoyment

needs. Due to passengers' life cost must be no worth calculation more than other service cost. When they choose to catch the airlines' any one airplane to fly to the another destination form the

country's airport. Hence, the influence of human factor in airport maintenance factor will influence any airlines' services feeling level to their passengers because human factor is one of the safety barrier which is used in order to prevent accidents or incidents of aircraft.

Therefore, the question is to which extent the error caused by human factor is included into the share of errors that are made during aircraft maintenance, such as flying

accidents, incidents, injuries, death, damages related to aircraft operation and maintenance. More airlines' detailed analyses have led to the knowledge that it is necessary to study the

interrelation of repair people, machines, airline factory maintenance and manufacturing working environment, and the air planes production processes. Human is the key factor production

process and in the process of operation of technical means since gives new value to the object of any one airplane manufacturing process.

As a factor, the human is not perfect and introduces unintentional error in the system. It is important to develop a system of ever identification and to work constantly on error

prevention. The works and activities on aircraft maintenance can produce hidden and active errors on the aircraft. Hidden errors are a type of errors that are seemingly invisible during aircraft

flying. Active errors are errors that occur immediately and result in immediate aircraft damage or injury , even death to any travelling passengers.

Hence, non human or without human factors will be less number to compare human factors to cause any flying incidents or accidents occurrence easily, e.g. damaging engine, old engine ( no renew engine), fire, crash etc. different kinds of causes. However, the main causes of human errors to cause any flying accidents may include: lack of communication between the pilot(s)

and airport airplane landing staffs, complacency ( assessment of work according to previous working experience), lacking of flying knowledge to the pilot, distraction, lack of

team work, fatigue, lack of materials and technological support), pressure on the work performer, lack of assertiveness ( lack of self-confidence or technical approach to work),stress ( working under pressure), lack of awareness etc. different human factors. Any one of above human factors will influence any flying accidents cause.

Moreover, instead of human factor, the flying working environment which refers to the space and place for work as well as the conditions of work factor will also influence human

error occurrence increasing chance, e.g. time pressure, equipment and tools enough number supplies, night shift, all of any one work environment factor will also influence human error

occurrence increasing chance in any flight flying. However, the factors that lead to cause of maintenance error may be caused from wrong information system supplies of equipment , aircraft

manufacturer, wrong working equipment and tools, wrong design of aircraft equipment and parts, incorrect working task arrangement, lacking technical education to the aircraft maintenance

workers, employee's bad personality, poor aircraft factory manufacturing working environment, poor airline company organization structure, working management and control and poor

communication etc. different manual or non manual factors.

Hence, all of above any one non manual factors will also raise manual error factor to cause any flying accidents occurrence chances. However, if any airlines hope to satisfy their passengers' flying service level. They must consider non manual and manual both factors for aircraft lean maintenance repair service aspect.


Influence of airside and off airport to airport geographical choice factor

What does airport airside means ? It includes a system of three components: runways, taxiways and agron-gate areas, on which aircraft and aircraft support vehicles operate. It brings this questions: Why can airport airside operation influence passengers feeling to the country's airport

and airline services? How does it influence airport ground service staffs' service performance?

In fact, this airside airport physical area choice has direct relationship between aircraft and apron gate areas of the terminal processing of passenger and cargo. They are major factors to influence operations on runway component. It means that airport ground service staffs' service efficiency, used for the passengers and air fright catching any airplanes processing.

Hence, in a geographical sense, landside and airside capacity on how designing and building og geographical area can bring indirect influence to passengers. They need to enter or indirect influence the airport , in special, many flights are staying on the airport runway as well as many passengers need to leave from the airplanes or enter to the

airplanes in the same time on the airport boundary. Hence, if the airport has good airside design , then many passengers will feel convenient to leave or enter the airport from the airside areas.

Airports are perhaps truly intermodel terminals in the transportatoin system. They provide an intersafe among air highway, rail and even water way travel. They are an important part of the medium and long distance intercity transportation system in our future transportation tools. Hence, it has enough reasons to support airside geographical airside and off airport factors can influence an airport and its airline flying service providers on its capacity as well as how it's capacity can influence passengers' satisfactory level when they arrive

the country's airport. Hence, airport's congestion growth problem that is needed to consider to any airports because when one airport 's congestion is growing.

It will influence passengers service satisfactory level to be fallen down in possible, e.g. capacity is increased by the addition of a new access road, such as additions provide a major increase.

Thus, the stair step growth, it will cause congestion growth because if the airport had used many areas for stair step growth and passengers will have less space to let them to walk on the ground and their airport congestion feeling will also increase when passengers are staying to leave the airport or waiting for check in or check out or waiting to transfer another airplane in the country's airport

The major airside factors to influence travelling passengers whose airport service feeling may include as below:

Availability of enough land for expansion for runways, availability of aids to navigation and air traffic control techniques that could result in reduction of separation between aircraft , noise, aircraft mix, load factor, exclusive use and use of gates , enough airside and outside facilities, availability of airspace, whether aircraft large size is enough capacity and where is location of gates, staffing, equipment freight, environmental protection regulation, and community attitudes toward airside operation.

Thus, whether the airport has enough facilities to satisfy passengers staying in its airport service need, it will have indirect influence further passengers increasing or decreasing

number problem. For example, if the airport terminal functions are spread over a large geographic area, access and facilities have to be expanded to accommodate the spread-out configuration of the terminal or if terminal facilities are grouped together, the access facilities can be congregated into a smaller geographical area.

The capacity of the landside is a function of the terminal design , which has a major influence on the relative to between airside and landside capacity. Also, these off airport factors can also

influence landside capacity, they may include: off airport parking, off airport terminals, urban development pattern, multiple jurisdiction, financial resources etc. issues. The sub factors of the off-airport access functions , they can influence passengers‘ services feeling to the airport. They may include: user and vehicle characteristics, e.g. occupants per vehicle, separate and preferential guide way subsystems, roadway traffic management, access link to major transportation , transportation connections. All of these airside and off-airport facilities will

influence passengers' servicing feeling when they arrive any countries‘ airports. Hence, any countries' airports ought not neglect any one of these minor airside facilities of inside airports to outside airports both.

The another geographical choice airport building issue, it is also one critical factor for how the development of airport cities. It will influence passengers‘ service feeling to any country airport. The questions may include: Why may any country need to develop an airport city? Can it bring economic benefit and attract many passengers to choose to travel the country? Can the airport city reform to raise airport service performance or service level? Airports have become new dynamic centers of economic activity, incorporating several commercial and

entertainment services inside passenger terminals, when developing a hotels and accommodations , office complexes, conference and exhibition centers or leisure facilities choices for

leisure passengers and business passengers both.

Airport-centered development may occur at different spatial scales ( from the micro scale of the passenger terminal to the regional or metropolitan scale), thus assuming different
shapes and mainfestations. Different concepts to address these developments can be found in the " airport city", airport corridor, and aerotopolis ( Guller, M. & Guller, M, 2003).

I shall explain how airport city concept can help to raise passenger service performance feeling in airports and airlines as below:

In general, airport passengers hope airports ought provide these different kinds service and achievement the lowest satisfactory service quality or performance level to let
them to feel, such as air transport needs have complex airport -neighborhood interactions ( in what concerns an eventual development towards the concept of airport city) requires the
identification of thes takeholders involved and an awareness of the relationships between them. Any airport's main task needs to provide traveling, air transport, shipping, entertainment services to
the dual market of airlines and travelers. As such, its primary interaction consists of the supply and demand relationship with the users stakeholder group ( passengers and airlines), which results in broad terms in the airports aeronautical revenues. Furthermore, non-aeronautical ( commercial) revenues also result from the interactions between airport and users, namely from agents such as cargo and passengers oriented organizations who pay rents or concession feeling to the airport authority, depending on the commercial arrangements binding these agents.

Thus, one successful airport city, it ought provide good neighborhood transport service to travelling passengers, e.g. bus, taxi, ferry etc. public transportation service. It aims to avail any airport passengers can catch any one of these public transportation tools to arrive airport or leave the airport easily. It also needs to provide hotel, conference service for business visitors as well as retail shops, cinemas for shopping visitors or entertainment visitors when they are staying in the country's airport(s). Also, it ought provide facilities to any cargo -oriented
organizations to deliver any cargo in short time rapidly. So, one airport's any neighborhood facilities have relationship to influence any passengers and airport organizations' service performance feeling between different user agents including: service provision ( e.g. between passengers and businesses), business transactions, supply and demand ( e.g. between public

transport providers and passengers and passengers or visitors) and employer-employee relationships ( businesses and workforce , such as airport airline ground service workers). Because if they feel that they can work in one comfortable airport working environment, they will feel happy and enjoyable to serve their passengers more everyday. It means that any airports' facilities will have indirect relationship to influence airport ground service workers' psychology to feel either enjoyable or hate to work in the airport environment often.

On conclusion, airports ought need to consider themselves airside and off airport facilities whether they have enough supplies and innovate their facilities to be better , even perfect in order to satisfy any airport visitors, travelers, user organizations and airport ground service employees to enjoy to work and use their services if they hope their service level or performance is satisfied

to their service needs for long term.

Influencing air connectivity to service quality factor

Can air connectivity growth decreases travel costs for attracting travelling passengers, consumers and businesses and facilities global productive growth? This seems to be particularly an issue when airport capacity is scare or when new airports are added to an existing airport system. What is air connectivity ?

Why does air connectivity raise passengers services? How to measure air connective service?

When direct and indirect connectivity relate to the airport connectivity available to local travelling passengers, any airports ought need to raise extra

airline services to raise service quality , e.g. cheaper air ticket price, in-flight service extra service provision, e.g. comfortable and clean and quiet air port waiting environment

service provision and feeling. However, passengers will generally prefer direct, non-stop connections over indirect air connectivity service.

Air connectivity service can assist airlines to raise competitive effort an offer and they provide access to the many destinations with too little demand for a direct flight, such as minimum connecting time differs in quality , due to in-flight time differences, the inconvenience and risk of missing a connection and transfer time for direct or indirect flights. Hence, any airlines can reduce passengers indirect or direct flight in-flight time to wait airplanes arrive to catch when they arrive any airports. This air inflight waiting time shorten service will attract many passengers to choose the airline to catch airplanes if its inflight waiting time to airport passengers is lesser than other airlines' in-flight waiting time in any airports. It can raise airline service quality, due to the airline has many passengers feel in-flight waiting time is shorten than other airlines often.

In fact, airport connectivity is one good concept method to raise passengers' satisfactory service level. One of the important factors for the connectivity of airports may include: The size

and economic strength of the local catchment area how drives outbound demand, size and economic activities as well as tourism attractiveness are an important cariable factor in explaining

inbound demand ( including the propensity to flying demand), landside accessibility drives the size of the catchment area that airlines can serve from a particular airport within a certain landside travel time, apart from the socio-economic variables factor, also cultural , political and the historical ties play a role in explaining demand the origin-destination level factor. All of the research on the factors that explain air level, demand at the origin-destination or airport level is widespread, including gravity modelling ( e.g. a bed at al., 2001) and regressions on aggregate

airport demand ( Dobruszkes, 2011). All of any one factors may be airport connectivity service to influence passengers' service feeling level in airports and airlines both service quality.

ON airport visit costs aspect, airlines also need to consider airport visit costs in their route development strategy. Visit costs may also influence passenger choice behavior when

airlines pass on higher/lower charges to the passenger through air fares. Although, airport visit costs generally represent a limited share of an airline's total operational costs, this share can be more significant for short haul flights as well as fair airlines. All of any one these airport charges and passenger fees variable may influence passengers airlines choice. They may include:

Fees variable, landing charge, parking charge for their vehicles or aircraft, passenger luggage charge, security charge, boarding bridge charge, noise charge, emission charge, airport development service increasing charge, check -in charge, terminal charge, cargo charge. So, if any one of these charges influence the airline ticket price rises, it will influence passengers' air ticket purchase choice to the airline in possible.

On airport service levels aspect, for keeping and attracting passengers, airlines and airports need to compete with services that improve the passengers experience. Such service

factors concern for immigration and luggage, but also relate to the terminals, waiting transfer another air plane time, shopping facilities, toilets, atmosphere and space cleaniness, friendliness of staff and availability of delicated lounges. Together they determine the image of an airport and its perceived value by passengers and airlines.

On airline routes development aspect, it can also influence passengers choices to the airline, e.g. Australia airline had developed long route to England destination. Any Australia

passengers can fly to England route directly. They do not need to transfer another air plane to go to England. Although, flying time is above 12 hours long time, but it can bring available to

passengers. They do not need to spend time to wait another air plane to transfer to go England in Australia any airports. THus, airline route development strategy airline planners require detailed, accurate information to make new route decisions, but airlines usually do not have the resources to fully evaluate every new route market. So, they need a sound well articulated business case, can convince airlines to introduce new air services, as well as airport / destinations can influence the airline planning process.

For example, Interviewer indicates that new routes are a huge investment and risk to an airline in airline economic view point, if the airline had not gathered any data to evaluate

whether the new route is worth to develop and predict passengers' new route choice behavior. It assumed 75% lead factor will influence any new route development in success. It indicates these different aircraft type and seats per flight, annual passenger requirements data for these aircrafts: Boeing 747 aircraft needs to satisfy 400 at least seats per flight and annual passenger requirement need 219, 000, aircraft airbus A340 aircraft needs 280 at least seats per flight and annual passenger requirements need 153,300 , Boesing 767 to 300 aircraft needs 220 at least seats per flight and annual passenger requirements need 120, 450 . Boeing 737 to 700 aircraft needs 76,650 and regional Jet aircraft needs 100 at least seats per flight and annual passenger requirements need 54,750.

Hence, any airlines need have route priorities strategy before they decide which new flight route(s) will be developed , in order to achieve airlines add service in order of expected profitability, different airlines have pursued different strategies, destinations can move up the priority board with: solid research and analysis ( always) and incentives (sometimes).However, any airline questions for new routes may include as below:

What is the current, actual market for a potential route?
How much can my airline stimulate the flight flying market?
How will the competition react?
How much market share will achieve?
How will be the connectivity contribution?
Will the new route be a financial success?

Hence, any airlines need to reduce uncertainty and risk, before they decide to develop any new route market.

The air service development process may include as below:

Step one: market assessment, required a quantify the time size of the existing air travel market

step two: strategy, deficiency analysis and detailed route analysis

step three: business case analysis, packaging and presenting the information to airlines

step fourth: evaluate and negotiate airline incentives

It is the final steps an appropriate incentive, in certain circumstances, helps airlines commit to new air service to satisfy any new route passengers' more satisfactory flying needs.

Similarly, the strategy steps follow: benchmark air services, identify deficiencies, identify new route opportunities, identify potential air service providers, assess viability of potential air services and prioritize route opportunities and target carriers.

Any airlines may find any information concerns new route business cases to decide their countries flying new routes choice , such as: catchment area profile: demographics, economy, tourist etc. information, airport profile : traffic and facilities information market profile; market sizes , top city pairs, traffic leakage etc. information, suggested service : frequency , schedule, airport routing information, route analysis: market share, load factor, stimulation potential, self-diversion etc. information, any airlines' past flying routes strategic considerations etc. information in order to predict and evaluate whether how many further passenger number is flying that they accept to choose the new flying routes travelling needs.

Hence, how to design to impact either the supply or demand for any new flight routes that is only important because of the country has less number of passengers accept to choose the new flying route to fly. Then, the new flying route does not needed to be design to supply to the country's travelling passengers because their acceptance to this new flying route ends are very less. However, the demand level is low new flying route needs to satisfy these three qualifying services criteria, such as: Are new routes only? Increase on existing routes? Does it work service rent incentives? Will the new flying route be satisfied to air service to the airline passengers and airport waiting passengers, e.g. strategically important? Marginally ( unprofitable) self-sustaining in the short term? New flying routes only? Increase an existing routes? Service rent incentives?

How can airports afford aggressive airline incentive / fee discounts and still fund route development marketing in a difficult economy? I recommend that the solution method may include new flying route design and developing and maximizing non-aeronautical revenue streams both, such as retail and duty free, food and beverage, parking , loyalty and premium programs and land development to airport building. Marketing funding strategy may be an ineffective incentive for travelling destinations. However, it may not differentiate a market, as route marketing incentives are used by over 80% of communities in the U.S. marketing incentives can be: Unilateral airport pays 100% or cooperative airlines matches some portion, funding amounts are often tied on the capacity of inbound seats to be available on the new flight ( flying) route. By calculating the economic impact of new visitors ( spend at the destination), a destination can calculate the return on investment in cooperative new flight ( flying) route market.

On conclusion, air connectivity is one important factor to influence any country's travelling passengers to the airline's service quality or service level in order to achieve new flying ( flight) route design , reducing inflight transfer another airplane waiting time in airport, or marketing development in success. So, any airlines can not neglect this air connectivity will influence their passengers' service quality.

Hence, air connectivity factor is also very important to influence any travelling passengers' service satisfactory level.


How to measure and rise airline

service quality

How are airline performing ? Nowadays, the rise of the low cost airlines' competition is serious, due to airlines hope to rise themselves attractions to influence passengers to choose to use their travelling services. So, different airlines have spend long time to build their unique person-to-person passenger services, which passengers use of different airlines, e.g. digital electronic air tickets purchase method. Any airlines hope to make each journey personalized to the individual will gain market share and improve its service quality to be more unique in order to reach the efforts of airlines to build high levels of customer service appears to have been generally noticed by passengers, when they choose to buy the airline's digital electronic ticket or paper air ticket to use its flying service.

Hence, improvement their digital e-ticket purchase experience and communications factor, for example, if any passengers can enter the airline's air ticket purchase website to buy electronic ticket to pre-book seats in the short time rapidly as well as there are enough seats number to supply to them to pre-book. So, they do not need to worry about without any seats to supply to them to catch the airline's flight to fly to anywhere in any time available conveniently. So, it seems that there is plenty of space for airlines to grow and improve their digital experience and communication method to let any passengers to feel, if the airline hopes to let its passengers to feel that it has unique service to compare others airlines.

The aviation industry plays a major role in the aspect of work and leisure to passengers around the global. So, nowadays passengers' demands to any airlines' service quality had been raised. Hence, any airline service industry messengers are under pressure to prove their services are customers oriented service improvement of performance that guarantees competitive advantages to the global travelling marketplace. So, it also implies that any airlines' services performance will be influenced to cause many passengers feel more poor and let passengers dissatisfy the airline's service performance. The, the airline will possible lose many passengers, due to passengers have many airlines choices, they can find any airlines to replace which any one airline to buy air ticket from internet at home immediately.

However, airlines' comfortable seats arrangement service provision feeling factor is still important in preferable to compare other factors, because passengers must need to sit any seats in any air planes. So, whether the air plane can provide new comfortable seats to let passengers to feel this factor is still the most important factor to influence any passengers to choose to the airline's air plane to catch. For example, service comfortability is how passengers observed the quality of service offered them by the airline's cleanliness, quiet zone, shops, restaurants and business pavilion in functioning like staffs, information desk, and in flight announcement are included as tangible features by the passengers ( Geraldine et a.,2013). All of these factors are needed often to measure whether their service performances are satisfactory to themselves passengers service needs.

Moreover, the other factors may include service affordability , it can be regarded as given passenger the opportunity to select from inclusive air ticket prices made available to the different group of passengers by the airlines, as a gesture of goodwill , to establish and reinforce customer loyalty and repeat purchases essential for the airline continuity as well as service reliability. it is the probability that airline will carry out its expected function satisfactory as stated in the flight schedule. Hence, there is a strong link between different airlines' service quality variables, airline image and repeat patronage from the passengers.

Service quality is a measure of how well the service level delivered matches passengers expectations to measure service quality based on input from focus groups. It consists of five factors ( tangibles, reliability, responsiveness, assurance and empathy). All of these factors will be identifies that how the airline service quality can be satisfactory to its passengers ' psychological and emotion enjoyable service needs.

Any one of these any five service factors will be important to influence the airline's passengers service feeling level to the airline. It means that the passenger will have more chance to choose the airline's service again ( repeating purchase its air ticket). Hence, any airlines can not neglect any one of service feeling to its passengers. It needs often to enquire questionnaires to evaluate whether its these five aspects of service quality , if it discovered any of these five aspects of service level is poor, e.g. 5 scale is the best service performance level, then it can attempt to find its error whether which aspects, it needs to very need to reach the 5 scale , the best service performance level when many passengers feel, e.g. enquiring 100 passengers who give 5 scale to reliability service aspect, before reliability service aspect has less than 50% passengers from 100 passengers who feel the airlines concerns this reliable service level aspect questions to be the best. It is one kind of measurement service quality method to any airlines.

Other service performance evaluation factor is satisfaction in the job to every airline front service or ground service staffs to the airline. Job satisfaction describes how content an employee is with his or her job. It is how the employee responses to a job. It can be considered as a part of life satisfaction to one organization, when the employee is working in the organization. Hence, if one airline front service as ground service staff who can feel more job satisfaction to compare his/her prior airline employer. Then, he/she won't be easy to change his/her present airline employer.

However, some factors can influence job satisfaction are pay and benefit, fair performance appraisal, career and promotional opportunities, proper reward and recognition, work-family life balance, the job itself, proper working conditions, leadership chance, autonomy in work.

Job satisfaction can also involve complex number of variables, circumstances, opinions and behavioral tendencies and a variety of work related outcomes, such as commitment, involvement, motivation, satisfaction, attendance. Hence, any airlines also need to concern how let their employees feel job satisfaction issue in order to avoid their leaving turnover number increases, due to job satisfaction and dissatisfaction depend on the expectations what the job supplies for an employee not the nature of the job.

Finally, instead of concerning employees job satisfaction issue, any airlines also need to concern passengers satisfaction issue because it will have any passengers will choose the airline, if it can bring more service satisfaction to let them to feel , then they will become repeat passengers to the airline.

What kinds of factors passengers were looking for and what were the reasons of choosing a specific airline? When one airline often is complained from its passengers. It will have more mistakes to let them to feel or dissatisfy its service. Hence the airlines needs to find which are its mistakes and improve in order to satisfy its passengers' expectations, e.g. finding what are the mistakes to the airlines' serious concern regarding passenger complaints and complaint satisfaction in order to make the airline more likely to meet its passengers' expectation in case of a problem. Hence, any airlines need to concern how to improve its employees' satisfactory service as well as its passengers' satisfactory service both issues as well as how to measure their service quality whether is enough to achieve general service acceptable performance to its passengers.

Reference

A bed, S. Y. A.O. Ba-Fail and S.M. Jasimuddin (2001), " An economatic analysis of international air travel demand in Saudi Arabia". Journal of air transport managmement, vol. 7, pp.143-148.

Bamber, L., & Dale, B.G. Lean production : a study of application in a traditoinal manufacturing environment. Production planning & control, 11 (3), 291-298, 2000.

Dobruszkes, F.M. Lennert and G. Van Hamme ( 2011). " An analysis of the determinants of air traffic volume for European metropolitan area". Journal of transport geographyy, vol. 19/4/pp.755-762.

Gealdine, O., & David , U.C. (2013). effects of airline service quality on airline image and passengers' loyalty: Findings from Arill Air Nigeria passengers, Journal of hospitality and management tourism, 4(2), 19-28. doi: http://dx.doi: 10.5897/HMT 2013, 0089.

Glass, R., Seifermann, S., & Metternich, J. The spread of lean production in the assembly, Process and maching industry. Procedia CIRP, 55, 278-283, 2016.

Guller, M. & Guller, M. (2003) From Airport to airport city. Editional Gustavo , Gili, Barcel on a.Intervistas Consulting Inc.

Massachusetts Institute Of Technology ( MIT), Lean Aerospace Initiative, Available: www.lean.mit.edu, 2005.